THE
HAND
PRINTED
HOME

THE HAND PRINTED HOME

35 stylish projects
using stencils,
lino cuts, and more

Jenny McCabe

CICO BOOKS
LONDON NEW YORK

Published in 2014 by CICO Books

An imprint of Ryland Peters & Small Ltd

519 Broadway, 5th Floor, New York NY 10012

20–21 Jockey's Fields, London WC1R 4BW

www.rylandpeters.com

10 9 8 7 6 5 4 3 2 1

A CIP catalog record for this book is available from the Library of Congress and the British Library.

ISBN: 978 1 78249 086 9

Printed in China

Editor: Hilary Mandelberg
Designer: Louise Leffler
Photographer: Emma Mitchell
Stylist: Nel Haynes
Illustrators: Step-by-step illustrations by Carrie Hill, print motifs by Jenny McCabe, and templates by Stephen Dew

For my fabulous family—Ben, Jesse, and Joe—with all my love

CONTENTS

INTRODUCTION

Printing by hand can be so much fun, and it's easier than you think to turn everyday things around the home into your own unique creations. Your handprinted designs can be applied to almost any surface—fabric, paper, ceramics, even your walls—and you don't always need any expensive specialist equipment.

This book contains 35 step-by-step projects that are designed to introduce you to lots of different handprinting techniques on many different surfaces. My aim is to share with you a selection of simple print motifs combined with easy sewing projects, and all the information you need to help you get started. You will soon be developing new skills and producing beautiful finished products.

As you work, allow time to experiment and test out the prints before you start on the final piece. Remember, though, that the beauty of handprinting lies in its imperfections and happy accidents, so give yourself time to play and let the designs develop. As with most creative processes, making mistakes is an important way to learn.

Hopefully, you will reach a point where you will be inspired to use your new skills to create your own designs. At that stage, it is worth knowing that you can achieve great designs just by using humble household objects such as potato mashers or rolling pins as your starting points.

As you get into handprinting, I hope that, like me, you will enjoy experimenting and seeing a simple shape become an amazing design. And if you sometimes you get that "blank canvas fear", just start making marks on a piece of paper. Your unique design will soon emerge.

Whether you are a complete novice without any knowledge of the techniques involved, or already have lots of creative experience, I hope my book will be a great starting point. But whichever category of reader you are, just play and have fun with printing and sewing. That's what I love to do!

PRACTICAL ADVICE

When choosing fabrics for the projects in this book, look for natural fabrics like canvas, calico, cottons, and linens. They are all are strong and hardwearing, and are easy to print and sew.

Before you begin printing, make sure you have a large flat surface to work on and always cover it with plenty of protective material, such as old newspaper, a plastic tablecloth, cut-up plastic refuse sacks, or an old shower curtain. Printing can get a bit messy.

INSPIRATION

Look at the world around you and see the patterns that are everywhere. Then, once you've become more observant, collect found images, clippings from magazines, color swatches, sketches, and doodles. These will all get your inspiration juices flowing.

Add to that making a sketchbook and doing lots of drawing. It's the best way to start your brain thinking about design. Whenever possible, try drawing with a paintbrush to help free up your lines and make the design process flow.

Experiment with color. Have a color wheel to hand so you can see the relationship between all the different colors, then try mixing your own fabric paints. Start by mixing just small amounts, noting down the ratios of each color that you have used.

Next, try out your color on the fabric you plan to use for your project. The color of the fabric has a habit of changing the color of the paint, especially once it's dry and ironed.

Once you have the perfect color, scale things up to make the amount you need for your project.

Ready to print? As well as using printing blocks made from your own designs, experiment by printing with found objects and layering these prints with your carved block prints to see what magic you can create.

Keep playing. The best designs appear from experimenting and just trying things out. For instance, try layering different colors, or repeating motifs in different ways. Use a mix of techniques—there's nothing to stop you having a base layer of shapes printed with a foam block and a detail layer screenprinted over the top. The more you play the more you'll be inspired.

HANDPRINTING TECHNIQUES

Handprinting is a very satisfying way to bring color and your own personal style into your home. All these techniques are designed to be fun and give great results, without the need for any previous experience. It doesn't matter which project you are making, the techniques are interchangeable. Mix and match the print techniques, designs, and sewing projects to find the perfect project for you. Have a go and learn some new skills.

FABRIC PAINTS

There are many different brands of fabric paint on the market. Some can be too runny to print with and lots come in tiny small bottles, which works out very expensive for large projects. Ask at your local art shop for advice on the best fabric paint for printing.

I find the most versatile way to work is by mixing my own standard acrylic artists' paints with acrylic fabric medium, which is available in any art-and-craft store. You mix the fabric medium 50:50 with your acrylic paint—and you've got fabric paint!

The resulting paint goes further and produces a softer finish on the fabric. It also means that the fabric can be washed. This technique is suitable for all the projects in the book—block printing, stencils, and screen-printing.

All fabric paints, including those made with acrylic fabric medium, must be heatset with an iron to fix them. Two minutes with a hot iron will usually be enough.

BASIC PRINTING EQUIPMENT

- Acrylic paint and acrylic fabric medium
- Old jars or plastic pots for mixing and storing paint
- Variety of paintbrushes
- Apron
- Scissors
- Craft knife
- Cutting board
- Newspaper
- Clean cloths
- Plenty of sponges, cut into small squares
- Sponge rollers
- Masking tape
- Pencil
- Tracing paper
- Hairdryer
- Iron
- Large flat surface for printing

TOP TIPS

● For every technique involving printing fabric you will need a large flat surface for printing that's protected from the fabric paints with old newspaper, a plastic tablecloth, cut-up plastic refuse sacks, or an old shower curtain.

● Always iron your fabric before printing so it lies flat and smooth.

● Set up your working space so the paints and sponges are well away from the fabric, to prevent any accidents.

● You can use a hairdryer to speed up the paint-drying process. When you are layering prints, you must dry each layer thoroughly before printing on top.

● Always iron your fabric to set the paint once the design is completed.

PRINTING WITH OBJECTS FROM AROUND THE HOUSE

You can print with just about anything from around your home. Think back to your schooldays, when you made hand- and vegetable prints, and prints using seashells and pasta. I have designed the projects in this book to remind you of what's possible, then you can go and play with things you find in your house and hopefully, come up with some exciting new designs.

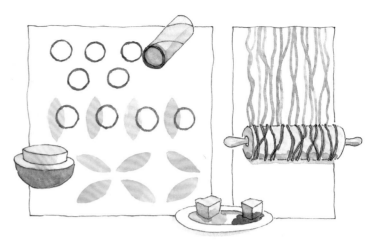

FRUIT AND VEGETABLE PRINTS

You can use lots of different vegetables to make prints with—think of the interesting contours you get when you cut an apple widthwise or a pepper lengthwise or widthwise. Fruit and vegetable printing is one of many forms of relief printing. You create a surface with raised areas that you cover with paint and print—these are the positive parts of the design—and you leave cut-away areas that remain unpainted and unprinted—the negative parts of the design.

The humble potato is one of the most versatile vegetables to use for printing because you can easily carve it to shape.

HOW TO POTATO PRINT

Cut a potato that is the right size for your project in half, width- or lengthwise, depending on your design. This will give you two surfaces to print with. Draw your motif onto the surface with a marker pen and cut away the areas that you don't need using a craft knife. You must cut downward at least ½in (1cm) into the surface to make sure your finished print has good, crisp edges. Pat the cut surface of your potato dry with kitchen paper, then sponge on the paint and press the potato onto the fabric to make your print. Remove carefully, reapply the paint, and you're ready to print again.

HOUSEHOLD ITEMS

Think of the way a coffee cup leaves a ring on your table. That's a print! Cardboard toilet-roll tubes, cookie cutters, and kitchen utensils like vegetable mashers or whisks all make interesting prints, too. Or you can use a wallpaper roller or rolling pin as your starting point.

HOW TO PRINT WITH HOUSEHOLD ITEMS

For a print from a household item that already has a sharp edge or a textured surface, simply dip the appropriate part of the item in fabric paint or apply the paint with a sponge, then you are ready to print. Clean the paint thoroughly off the household item after use.

Alternatively, you can cover a roller with shapes cut from foam sheets with a peel-off sticky backing (see the Japanese Fabric Gift Wrap on page 112,) or you can wrap the roller in string. Apply the paint with a sponge and whizz the roller across the surface to create a random striped print or a pattern that's a mesh of lines. Once again, this technique uses a relief printing technique (see above left). Experiment, play—and see what you can come up with.

Extras you will need for printing with objects from around the house

Fruits, vegetables, and household items; marker pen; foam sheets with a peel-off sticky backing; string

STAMPS

You can create reusable stamps for printing from a variety of different materials, such as erasers, foam sheets, and lino. These all use the relief printing technique. You cut the material away to make the positive and negative parts of the design.

The best way to transfer a design onto a stamp is to trace the image onto tracing paper, then place the tracing paper face down on your stamp. Rub the back of the tracing paper and the image will be transferred onto your stamp. The image will now be reversed but once you print it, it will be the correct way around.

CARVED ERASER STAMPS

Erasers come in all shapes and sizes and provide you with a nice, flexible surface to print from. You can use the shape of the eraser—the dot formed by a pencil eraser or a small eraser, for example—or you can carve a large eraser into the shape and detail you need.

HOW TO USE ERASER STAMPS

1 For a carved eraser, mark your design on the surface of the eraser and use a lino cutter and craft knife to cut away the negative areas of the design—the areas that you don't want to print.

2 Cut away the excess eraser from around the design so your finished print has good, crisp edges, but leave enough of the eraser to hold onto from behind.

3 Sponge on the paint and press the eraser stamp onto the fabric to make your print. Carefully remove the eraser stamp and reapply the paint to make the next print.

4 For printing a simple polka-dot design, you can use the eraser on the end of a pencil—it is a ready-made stamp!

Eraser stamps will last a long time if you wash them after use, store them without stacking them on top of one another, and don't try and use them again as erasers.

LINO STAMPS

You can buy sheets of lino in many different sizes from art shops. Invest in a good set of sharp lino-cutting tools; they will make your life easier when it comes to carving your design.

HOW TO USE LINO STAMPS

1 Transfer the design onto the piece of lino and carefully carve it out. Use very sharp tools, always cut away from your body, and take great care. Practice on a small piece of lino first if you've never tried lino-cutting before. A good tip is to warm your lino before carving it, as it makes it softer. I sit on mine!

2 You need to cut downward to at least half the depth of the lino to make sure your finished print has good, crisp edges. You don't need to carve away all the lino around your design; just carve up to ½in (1cm) all around, then cut away the excess using scissors.

The raised areas are those that you will cover with paint and print (the positive parts of the design) and the carved-away areas will remain unpainted (the negative parts of the design).

3 If your design is very intricate, it helps to cut the carved motif out completely and stick it to a wooden or acrylic backing block. That way you have something solid to hold onto and the carved lino won't be damaged.

4 Once you think your lino stamp is ready, do a test print. If there are printed areas where there shouldn't be, carve away the excess lino.

Repeat this process until you are happy with the way the stamp is printing. You can apply your paint to the lino stamp with a sponge roller or by dabbing it on with a sponge.

5 Print onto the fabric by placing your lino stamp, paint side down. Use a clean roller or brayer to roll firmly across the back. Carefully peel the lino stamp off and reapply paint, ready to make the next print.

Lino stamps will last a long time if you wash them after use and store them flat.

FOAM STAMPS

Making printing blocks with foam sheets is an inexpensive and fun way to create stunning prints. You can easily buy foam sheets online or in the children's section of a stationery or art store.

Once you have cut the foam into the shape of your motif, you stick it onto a rigid backing—a wooden block, a wine coaster, or an acrylic block—to give you something to hold onto. The foam shape is the positive, raised part of the design that you coat with paint, while the block becomes the negative, unprinted area.

When printing certain designs, it helps to be able to see through the backing block to line up your prints. In that case, it's best to use an acrylic backing block.

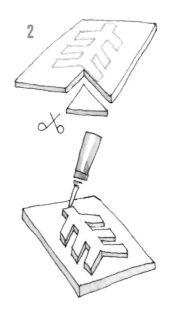

HOW TO USE FOAM STAMPS

1 Transfer your design onto your sheet of foam. Take care when doing this as any small marks or indentations on the foam will show up in the finished print. On the other hand, you can use this to your advantage, scoring the foam deliberately to make a fine line or pushing the tip of a pencil in to make spots. However, don't crease the foam or make too many pencil lines if you want a good, clean print.

2 Cut out your foam shapes either with scissors or a craft knife and stick them to your backing block.

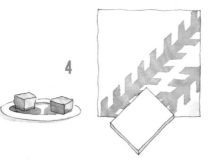

3 When cutting intricate designs, I sometimes like to use foam sheets with a peel-off sticky backing. I stick a whole piece of foam sheet to the block first, then cut out the design and peel away the unwanted foam. You can also use ready-cut foam shapes—the principle is the same.

4 Once your foam stamp is ready, use a sponge or a sponge roller to lightly coat the surface with paint. If you accidentally get any paint on the backing block, remove it with a clean cloth before you print. Place the stamp face down on the surface and press firmly and evenly on the back. Carefully remove the stamp and reapply the paint before the next print.

Foam stamps can be reused many times and will last well if washed carefully after use and if not stacked up together, as this will flatten the foam.

Extras you will need for printing with stamps

Erasers; lino sheets; foam sheets with a peel-off sticky backing; wooden or acrylic backing blocks; lino-cutting tools; roller or brayer

STENCILS AND SCREEN PRINTS

Stencils and screen prints are forms of resist printing. In this type of printing, part of the design "resists" or blocks the paint and prevents it coming into contact with certain parts of the surface being printed. Stencils and screen prints give a positive print so there is no need to worry about producing a design in reverse.

STENCILS

Stencils can be made from many different materials—paper, thin sheets of plastic, and masking tape are some examples. The stencil will "resist" the paint and prevent some areas from being printed.

Freezer paper is a plastic-coated kitchen paper that's great for stencils. If you place it shiny side down on fabric and iron over it, it will adhere to the fabric long enough for you to print. Alternatively, you can cut an ordinary paper stencil and use repositionable spray glue to hold it in place.

HOW TO USE A STENCIL

1 Draw your design onto the paper, leaving a wide border around the edge of the design. Cut out the design using a craft knife. If you are planning on a repeat design that is intended to cover a large area, you should cut several stencils the same as they will begin to clog up and degrade after a few uses.

2 Position your stencil on the fabric and sponge lightly or use a sponge roller to evenly coat the surface with fabric paint. Take care not to move the stencil as you apply the paint.
3 Leave to dry or use a hairdryer to speed up the drying, then remove the stencil. If you are working with a repeat design, reposition the stencil and sponge with paint again.

MASKING TAPE STENCILS

Using masking tape to create a stencil to "resist" the paint is one of the easiest ways to transform an object or a piece of fabric.

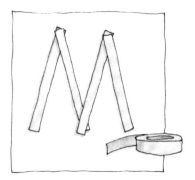

HOW TO USE MASKING TAPE STENCILS

Make sure that your fabric is ironed and flat or, if you are working with a painted surface, that it is clean and dry, with no flaking paint. Mark out your design with chalk if necessary, then apply the tape. Stick it down firmly, making sure the edges don't conceal any bubbles or gaps, or the paint will bleed underneath. Depending on your design, you can either mask off all the areas in one go, or you can mask one part at a time. If you want to apply the paint in layers/stages, make sure it is thoroughly dry before moving on to masking for the next layer/stage. When you have finished, carefully remove all the tape and dry your paint completely before ironing the fabric.

SCREEN-PRINTING

This is another type of stenciling. It involves using fine mesh fabric tightly stretched over a wooden or metal frame. You can attach a stencil to the screen to "resist" the paint, or use screen filler together with screen drawing fluid, or you can use screen filler on its own.

You can easily try various methods of screen-printing fabric at home without the need for expensive equipment. You can even make your own screen-printing frame (see page 16). The projects in this book are designed to give you the opportunity to try all the methods.

After using any of the screen-printing techniques, always allow the fabric paint to dry before ironing to heat-set it. Wash your screen immediately after use: never leave the paint to dry on the screen as it will ruin it.

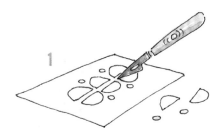

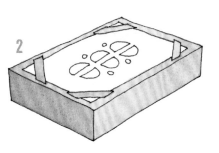

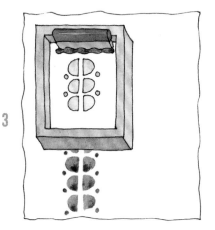

HOW TO SCREEN PRINT USING A STENCIL

1 Prepare your paper stencil by drawing your design in the center, the image should fit within the area of the mesh, make sure you leave a border of 4in (10cm) of blank paper around the image. Cut it out with a craft knife.

2 Turn your screen mesh-side up and place your paper stencil on top. Use parcel tape to attach the stencil and to cover any parts of the screen not covered by the stencil.

3 With your fabric on a flat surface, place the screen, stencil-side down, on top. Put a generous blob of paint on the screen above the image, then, using a squeegee the width of your screen, firmly and evenly drag the paint across the surface. Repeat twice more, then carefully lift up the screen and reposition it ready for the next print.

HOW TO PRINT USING SCREEN DRAWING FLUID AND SCREEN FILLER

The following instructions apply when using any screen-printing frame, but here we show a home-made one (see page 16).

1 With the screen mesh-side down and a soft pencil—to avoid tearing the mesh—draw your motif onto the mesh. Leave a wide border around the edges of the motif.

2 Turn the screen mesh-side up and use a paintbrush and screen drawing fluid to paint over the penciled lines of the motif. You need to achieve a good solid line—if the line is too thin, the screen drawing fluid will wash out when you apply the screen filler, leaving parts of your design missing.

3 Leave the mesh to dry fully; you can use a hairdryer on a low heat if necessary.

4 Once the mesh is dry, coat your screen with screen filler. Do this with an old credit card or squeegee. Pour a blob of screen filler on the card and drag it across the screen, covering the surface with a thin, even coat. Take care not to overdo this or the drawing fluid will start to dissolve. Just

drag the card quickly and smoothly once or twice across the screen.

5 You don't need to go right to the edges of the screen as these will be covered with parcel tape later on. Leave to dry completely, using a hairdryer on a low heat to speed things up.

6 Once the filler is completely dry, wash out the drawing fluid under running water. Allow the whole screen to dry, then prepare your screen for printing by covering the edges with parcel tape so no paint can get through to the fabric in areas where it shouldn't.

7 With the screen mesh-side down, put a generous blob of fabric paint on top and, using the credit card or squeegee, scrape the paint across the surface of the screen in one steady action.

8 Repeat a couple more times, then carefully lift up the screen and reposition it for the next print.

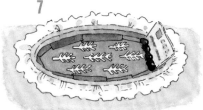

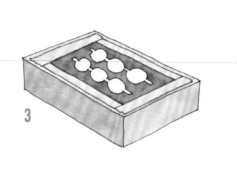

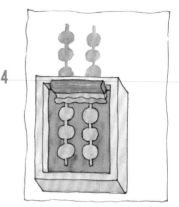

HOW TO SCREEN PRINT USING SCREEN FILLER ON ITS OWN

1 With the screen mesh side down and a soft pencil—to avoid tearing the mesh—draw your motif onto the mesh. Leave a wide border around the edges of the motif.
2 Turn the screen mesh side up and paint around your motif with an even coat of screen filler. Once the filler is dry, it will act as a barrier—or "resist"—stopping any

fabric paint seeping through onto the fabric in those areas. You don't need to paint right to the edges of the screen, just up to 2in (5cm) all around the motif.
3 Leave to dry fully; you can use a hairdryer to speed things up if you like. Once the filler is completely dry, cover the edges of the screen with parcel tape.

4 Lay your screen mesh-side down on the fabric. Using a credit card or squeegee, firmly and evenly drag the paint across the surface of the screen in one steady action.
5 Repeat a couple more times back and forth, then carefully lift up the screen and reposition it for the next print.

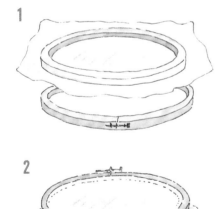

HOW TO MAKE YOUR OWN SCREEN-PRINTING FRAME

1 You can make your own screen-printing frame using a two-part embroidery hoop and some very fine nylon fabric—either net curtain fabric or screen-printing fabric from a specialist supplier. Simply cut the fabric so it is about 4in (10cm) larger all around than the embroidery hoop. Place the mesh over the inner ring of the hoop, position the outer ring on top and tighten the screw.
2 Work around the hoop, pulling the mesh tight as you go. Continue tightening the screw until the mesh is well stretched and securely held in place. Use parcel tape to cover the edges, leaving enough room for your print motif in the center.

Extras you will need for printing with stencils and screen prints
Paper and repositionable spray glue or freezer paper; parcel tape; readymade screen-printing frame or an embroidery hoop and fine nylon mesh fabric; squeegee or old credit card; screen filler; screen drawing fluid; parcel tape; access to running water

DIGITAL PRINTING

There are different printing papers available that allow you to take images from the computer and transfer them to fabrics, ceramics, and other surfaces. I have created projects that will let you try out these techniques—then you can use them with your own designs.

PHOTO TRANSFERS

You can use drawing software on your computer to draw artworks, or use a photo-editing program to get photos ready to print out onto special inkjet photo transfer paper. Photo transfers will print back to front, so remember to reverse your photos before printing them out.

HOW TO USE PHOTO TRANSFERS

1 Use your computer program to prepare your photo. Make it the required size and flip it so it is back to front. This is especially important if your photo has text on it. Failure to flip the photo will mean that your text will be a mirror image when it is printed.
2 Print your photo onto the right side of the photo transfer paper and cut it out, leaving a narrow border.

3 Place the paper, photo side down, on the fabric. Following the instructions that came with your paper, iron your transfer in place.
4 Peel away the backing to reveal the photo bonded to the fabric.
5 Do not iron directly on top of the bonded photo and take care when washing. Always follow the manufacturer's instructions to be extra sure.

CERAMIC TRANSFERS

Transferring images to ceramics and glass at home is easy when you use inkjet decal paper. You print out your image onto the special paper (there's no need to reverse the image), transfer it to your item, then bake it in the oven for a short time. The finish is not dishwasherproof, so this technique isn't recommended for mugs and cups, but is perfect for a vase or storage jar.

HOW TO USE CERAMIC TRANSFERS

1 Prepare the image on your computer and set the size and colors. Print the image onto the shiny (right) side of your inkjet decal paper, following the manufacturer's instructions.
2 Leave the ink to dry, then spray the paper with a few coats of clear varnish. The varnish will protect the ink from running when you place your transfer in water. Spray outside or in a well-ventilated area and leave to dry fully between coats.

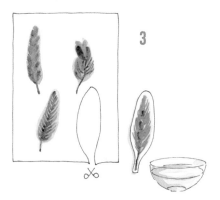

3 Cut out your image, leaving a very narrow border around the edge. Place the transfer in a bowl of clean water and leave for 30 seconds or until you can feel the backing paper starting to slide off when you move it between your thumb and finger.
4 Leaving the backing in place, remove the transfer from the water and position it on your ceramic or glass item. Smooth the transfer down while gently sliding out the backing paper. Smooth the transfer with your finger to remove any air bubbles.
5 Once the transfer is in position, with no bubbles or creases, place the item in a preheated oven, following the manufacturer's instructions. The recommended temperature is usually 130°C/250°F/Gas ½. Once it has cooled, your item is ready to use.

Extras you will need for digital printing
Inkjet photo transfer paper; inkjet decal paper; inkjet printer; clear spray varnish

HONEYCOMB BUNTING

Bunting is great for brightening up a space. This bee-themed bunting is sure to bring some sunshine into your home. You can make your bunting as long as you need by adding more triangles.

LEVEL:

PRINTING TECHNIQUE

Foam stamp

MATERIALS

Main fabric: approx. 28 x 12in (70 x 30cm)

Lining fabric: approx. 28 x 12in (70 x 30cm)

Pencil, ruler

Bias binding: 99in (2.5m)

PRINTING TOOLS

Print motifs on page 117

Foam sheets

Scissors

Wooden or acrylic backing block

Glue

Sponge or sponge roller

Fabric paint in three colors

1 Iron your fabrics and cut them to size. Draw your triangles on the fabrics using a pencil and a ruler. My triangles are 8in (22cm) along the top edge and 8in (22cm) from the center of the top edge to the point. To fit in as many triangles as possible, rotate every other triangle through 180 degrees, but leave a 1in (25mm) gap in between your triangles.

2 This project was created using three different shades of orange fabric paint and three foam-sheet printing blocks—one for printing the bee, one for the hexagon outlines, and one for the solid hexagons. The design is applied using the foam stamp technique on page 13. Prepare your stamps using the bee and hexagon motifs on page 117. Load each stamp with one of the fabric paints using a sponge, and build up your design on the main fabric triangles. Practice first on a scrap of fabric until you are confident you can achieve a clean, clear print.

3 You can make a repeated pattern with your hexagons or just place them randomly on the triangles. Print at least 2 triangles with each of your blocks so you have an even number of different triangles for your bunting. Your motifs can overlap the edges of the triangles.

4 When you are happy with your design, iron the fabric to set the paint, then cut out all your printed triangles and your lining triangles.

5 Place a printed triangle and a lining triangle right sides together. Using a ⅜ in (1cm) seam allowance, sew around the two long sides, then trim away the point, taking care not to cut through the stitching. Turn the triangle right-side out and press. Repeat with all your triangles.

6 To join your triangles together to make a strip of bunting, press your bias binding in half all along its length.

7 Leaving the first 10in (25cm) of bias binding clear, place the unstitched side of your first triangle in between the folded binding. Pin in place. Sew along the edge of the bias binding to keep the triangle in place, then continue adding all the triangles in the same way, leaving a 3in (8cm) gap between each one. Leave 10in (25cm) at the other end of the binding for hanging.

3

5
7
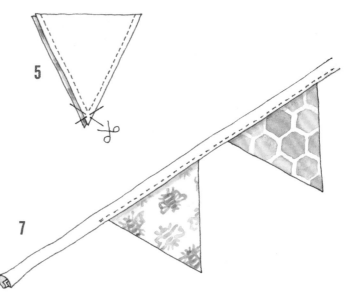

TIE-TOP CURTAINS

These lovely curtains hang from easy ribbon ties with beautiful button embellishments. When you measure the width of your windows, add lots of extra fabric to make sure you get a soft, floaty effect.

PRINTING TECHNIQUE

Stencil screen print

MATERIALS

Fabric: cut two pieces (see instructions)

Extra for ties or ribbon (see instructions)

Buttons (see instructions)

Pins, needle, matching thread, tape measure

PRINTING TOOLS

Print motif on page 118

Letter-size (A4) screen

Sheet of letter (A4) paper

Craft knife

Parcel tape

Fabric paint

Squeegee

Hairdryer

1 Start by measuring your window. If you would like your curtains to be floaty and full, use double the window width. Whether you do this or not, add 1½in (4cm) to the width and 4in (10cm) to the top and bottom for your edges and hems. Cut out two pieces of fabric to the measurements you require.

2 The design is applied using the screen-printing technique on pages 14–15. Prepare your stencil using the stem-and-leaves motif on page 118. Place the motif in the very center of a letter-sized (A4) sheet of paper. The image should fit within the area of the mesh. Make sure you leave a border of 4in (10cm) of blank paper around the image. Cut it out and tape it to the mesh side of your screen.

3 Iron your fabric and lay it on a flat surface ready for printing. If your curtains are very long, you will have to print in sections, moving the fabric from time to time.

4 Lay your screen mesh-side down where you want the first print to go. Add a generous blob of fabric paint to the top of the screen, just above the design. Using the squeegee, scrape the paint across the surface of the screen in one steady action. Repeat a couple more times back and forth, then carefully lift up the screen. Dry your print with a hairdryer. Practice first on a scrap of fabric until you are confident you can achieve a clean, clear print.

2

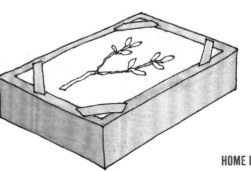

5 Continue printing your fabric in this way to build up your design. Let each print dry before moving the screen to its next position. Once you have covered your fabric, leave the paint to dry fully, then iron the fabric to set the paint.

6 Next, decide how many pairs of evenly spaced ties you want at the top of your curtains. They need to be at least 10in (26cm) long and you need two ties at each point. You can use ribbons or make narrow fabric strips.

7 To make fabric strips, cut your fabric to 12 x 2½in (30 x 6cm), fold and press the sides and one short edge by ½in (1cm), then fold over lengthwise to join the long sides. Sew closed with a neat line of topstitches along both sides and the top (see page 116 for tips on making fabric ties).

8 To neaten the sides of the curtains, fold the edges over to the wrong side by ½in (1cm), press, then fold the edges again by ½in (1cm). Press again, then stitch neatly along the first fold.

9 Neaten the tops of the curtains by folding them first by ½in (1cm), then by 2in (5cm). Pin in place.

10 Now you can attach your ties to the tops of the curtains. Tuck them in pairs, facing downward and evenly spaced, under the pinned hem. Stitch neatly along the first fold, securing all the ties and closing the hem.

11 Fold the ties upward and sew another line of stitches along the top edge. This secures the ties in their final position and adds extra strength.

12 Hand-sew a button to the front of the curtains at the bottom of each pair of ties, for decoration.

13 To hem the bottom of the curtains, hang them in position at the window and pin up the bottom of each so they match. Take the curtains down and fold the edge over to the wrong side, first by ½in (1cm), then by 2in (5cm). Press, then sew in place to finish.

5

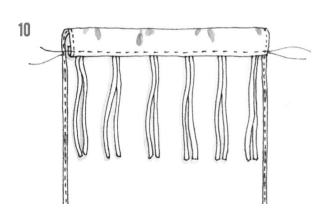

10

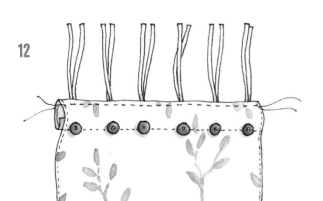

12

WALL PRINTING

Printing directly onto a wall is a great way to transform any space. You can be as ambitious or as conservative as you like—print the whole wall or just a small area.

LEVEL:

PRINTING TECHNIQUE

Foam stamp

MATERIALS

A wall!

PRINTING TOOLS

Print motifs on page 121

Foam sheets

Craft knife

Scissors

Wooden or acrylic backing blocks

Glue

Chalk or masking tape (optional)

Acrylic paint in a variety of colors

Sponge

Paintbrush (optional)

1 Make sure the wall you are going to print on is clean, dry, and as smooth as possible. A wall painted with matt emulsion is best. Gloss paint is slippery to work on and woodchip and bare brick will be very tricky and will give poor results.

2 If you need to paint the wall before you start, make sure to leave 24 hours before you print so the paint is completely dry.

3 The design is applied using the foam stamp technique on page 13. Prepare your stamps using the three insect motifs on page 121.

4 Plan out your printing pattern before you begin. You can do this by eye or by measuring. Use chalk or little strips of masking tape to mark the positions of each motif. If you are covering a large surface, stand back and check that the placement is right.

PRINTING TIPS

Be extra-careful that the stamp doesn't slip when printing on the wall. Hold onto it well. You can touch up your prints with a small paintbrush to cover up any imperfections.

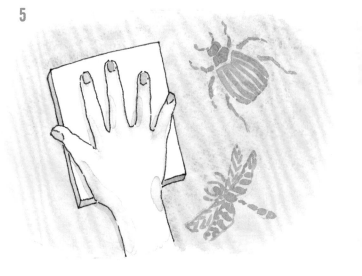

5 Once you are happy with your design, you can begin to print. Load the stamp with paint using a sponge. Take care not to use too much paint or the stamp will slip and slide on the wall and you won't get a perfect print. If at all possible, do a test print somewhere on the wall that won't be visible (for example, behind a mirror, or a framed picture). This will help you to see how it feels to print on a wall.

6 Print your motifs one at a time, working first with one color across the whole area, then changing colors to build up the rest of the design. I have overlaid some of my prints with a second color to give the design more definition. To do the same, simply wait for the first color to dry, then load your stamp with your second color and carefully line up and print over the top. This is where acrylic backing blocks really help because you can see exactly where your print is going.

7 Once you have printed all your motifs, allow them to dry naturally. Acrylic paint is as durable as wall paint and does not need heat-setting or sealing with varnish.

5

ROLLER BLIND

Bring a plain blind to life with a simple handprinted pattern. Match your decor with the colors and print that you choose.

LEVEL:

PRINTING TECHNIQUE

Stencil

MATERIALS

Roller blind

PRINTING TOOLS

Print motifs on page 118

Freezer paper

Craft knife

SpongeFabric paint

PRINTING TIPS

You can make these stencils out of three long lengths of freezer paper that fit right across the blind. That way you only have to print three times once you have done all the cutting out!

1 This design is applied using the stencil technique on page 14.

2 Prepare your stencils by first measuring the width of the blind. Cut out three lengths of freezer paper about 8in (20cm) longer than this measurement.

3 You are going to build up your printed design in three bands — a bottom band consisting of large motifs, then a band of middle-sized motifs, then finally a top band of small motifs. Prepare your three stencils using the motifs on page 118. Trace each motif repeatedly onto the freezer paper so you end up with the three bands you need to print. Make sure not to trace motifs too close to the edges of the freezer paper. Once you are happy with your design, use a craft knife to cut out the three stencils.

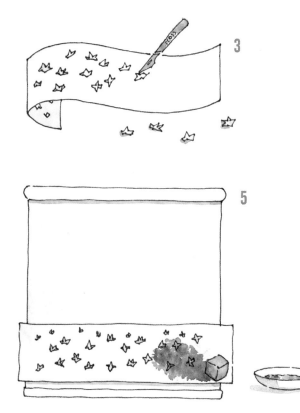

4 Unroll your blind and lay it on a large, flat surface ready for printing. Position your first stencil across the bottom of the blind on the right side and iron it in place.

5 Sponge the fabric paint onto the blind through the stencil. Practice first on a scrap of fabric until you are confident you can achieve a clean, clear print. Once the paint is dry, peel the stencil away very carefully.

6 Next position the middle stencil just above the first row of prints and repeat the sponging process. Again, once the paint is dry, peel the stencil away carefully. Finally, position the top stencil and sponge on the fabric paint, this time sponging on less paint from bottom to top to give the impression of the motif fading away (see photo opposite for reference).

7 Once the whole blind is dry, iron it on a low heat to set the fabric paint and hang the blind at the window.

PRINTING TECHNIQUE

Masking tape stencil

MATERIALS

Nest of tables

Clear varnish or stain (optional)

PRINTING TOOLS

Tape measure

Set square

Chalk

Craft knife

Masking tape

Newspaper

Scissors

Spray paint in a contrasting color to your tables

Clear spray varnish

NEST OF TABLES

Upcycling old furniture is a great way to give new life to a piece of furniture you have fallen out of love with. This idea capitalizes on the natural color and grain of the wood. These show through, making them part of the design, but you could also follow the same technique using a painted item.

1 This design is applied using the masking tape stencil technique on page 14. Make sure the furniture you are going to stencil has a clean, dry surface. If it needs to be revarnished or stained, do this at least 24 hours in advance.

2 This design was laid out by eye, not by measuring perfectly. Use a set square only as a rough guide; don't spend too much time worrying about precise measurements. Divide the surface of your piece with equally spaced vertical lines marked in chalk. It doesn't matter how far apart they are, as long as they are equally spaced. Now mark dotted lines parallel to and centrally between the first lines.

3 Cut the end of a piece of masking tape perfectly square and attach it so its bottom left corner is lined up with one of the dotted lines. Cut the other end of the tape so it is perfectly square and its top edge is lined up with the nearest vertical line. Now stick a second piece of masking tape over the left-hand end of the first piece and at a 90-degree angle to it. The second piece of masking tape will meet the vertical line to its left at a 45-degree angle. This gives you your first "V".

4 Continue adding lengths of masking tape in the same way until the surface of the piece is covered with zigzags. Worry less about accuracy and more about the overall design looking straight. The spacing between the zigzags is up to you—just try to make it the same all over. Continue your masking tape over the edges of the piece of furniture and make sure it is stuck down securely so you get nice crisp edges to your painted design.

5 Use newspaper attached with masking tape to cover any parts of the furniture you don't wont to get paint on—in this case, the table legs.

6 Prepare an area for spray-painting. It's best to spray-paint outside or in a very well-ventilated area. I used gold spray paint, as I thought it complemented the dark wood of my tables, but if you have a light-colored wood, a darker color of spray paint would work better. Spray your prepared furniture with two or three light coats of spray paint or until you are happy with the color and coverage you have achieved. Leave to dry completely, following the paint manufacturer's instructions.

7 Slowly peel away all the tape, taking great care not to peel away the paint or damage the original surface. If you need to touch up any areas, do so by spraying a small amount of the paint into a disposable pot, then use a paintbrush to touch up the areas that need it. If required, you can lightly scrape away any small bleeds of paint with a craft knife. Once you are happy with the design, again working outside or in a well-ventilated area, spray a few coats of clear varnish over the surface of the furniture—and you have finished.

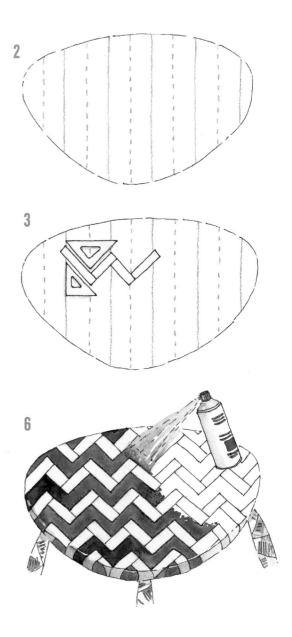

2

3

6

PRINTING TIPS

This is a clever and simple way of setting out a design, using the width of the masking tape as the basis of your pattern.

LEAFY LAMPSHADE

Lampshade kits are readily available and come in all shapes and sizes. This project is for a small drum lampshade—a great first lampshade project that will brighten up any room. It's not as tricky as you may think. Alternatively, you could revamp an old lampshade by recovering it with your newly printed fabric.

LEVEL: 🐦 🐦

PRINTING TECHNIQUE

Foam stamp

MATERIALS

Lampshade kit

Fabric (see lampshade kit for size required)

Scissors

Stiff card (optional)

PRINTING TOOLS

Print motifs on page 119

Foam sheets

Scissors

Wooden or acrylic backing block

Glue

Fabric paint in three colors

Sponge

1 Before you begin, check the size of fabric required for your kit, if using. Iron your fabric and cut it out, making it slightly larger than the required size. Lay it on a flat surface ready for printing.

2 The design is applied using the foam stamp technique on page 13. Prepare your stem of leaves stamps using the motifs on page 119.

3 Load each stamp with one of the fabric paints using a sponge, and build up your design on the fabric by overlapping the leaves. Practice first on a scrap of fabric until you are confident you can achieve a clean, clear print.

4 When you are happy with your design, iron the fabric to set the paint. You're now ready to begin assembling your lampshade.

3

PRINTING TIPS

This design is made up of a simple stem of leaves, one in solid color and the other in outline. Layering the two together in a random way and using different shades of paint will give you an interesting print with lots of depth.

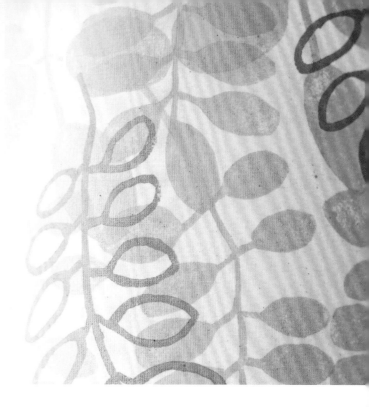

5 If you are using a lampshade kit, make sure you familiarize yourself with the accompanying instructions. Kits come with 2 metal rings to form the top and bottom of the lamp, a roll of heat-resistant plastic with a peel-off sticky backing for reinforcing your fabric, double-sided tape to stick the rings to the fabric, and a finishing tool for tucking away the raw edges.

6 Lay your fabric out, printed side down. Peel off the first 4in (10cm) of the backing from the plastic. Starting at one end of your fabric and peeling off the backing gradually, stick the plastic to the fabric, making sure you smooth out the plastic and fabric as you go. Trim your fabric to the recommended size according to the kit instructions.

7 Next, prepare your metal lampshade rings by attaching the double-sided tape all the way around both rings. Remove the backing tape on both rings and place them on either edge of your fabric at one end. Make sure the light fitting is pointing towards the inside of your lamp and is on the correct side, depending on how you intend to use the lampshade. If it is going to be for a pendant light, the fitting will need to be at the top of the lamp but if you are going to use it on a lamp base, it will need to be at the bottom. Slowly roll both rings at once along the edges of the fabric to stick the fabric to the rings.

8 Just before you get to the end, add a strip of double-sided tape along the final edge of the fabric. Remove the backing paper, then continue rolling the rings to stick the final edge of the fabric in place.

9 Fold the excess fabric at the top and bottom of the lampshade over the metal rings. Use the finishing tool provided in the kit or pieces of stiff card to tuck away any raw edges—and you're done.

5

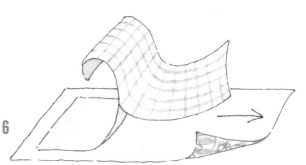

6

8

9

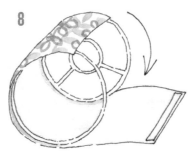

CERAMIC DECAL PRINTING

Transform plain ceramic items into your own stunning designer pieces using your inkjet printer and the very clever inkjet decal paper.

LEVEL:

PRINTING TECHNIQUE

Ceramic transfer

MATERIALS

Ceramic item

PRINTING TOOLS

Print motifs on page 120

Letter-sized (A4) inkjet decal paper

Clear spray varnish

Hairdryer

Scissors or craft knife

PRINTING TIPS

This technique has endless possibilities as you can use any artwork you like. Use your computer's graphics/photo program to prepare your images and print them to scale on the special paper. You don't need to reverse the image.

1 This design is applied using the ceramic transfer technique on page 17. Your finished ceramic item will be fairly durable but cannot go in a dishwasher and will not survive too much scrubbing. Decorate something like a vase or a storage jar that will not require much washing.

2 Scale up the motifs on page 120 to the sizes you need for your ceramic item and print them onto the shiny side of your inkjet decal paper.

3 Once the ink is dry, spray the paper with a thin, even coat of clear varnish. Use a hairdryer to dry the varnish, then repeat to add two more thin coats. The varnish will protect your ink from running when you place your decal in water in step 5.

4 When the varnish is completely dry, cut out the decals using scissors or a craft knife. Leave the narrowest border possible.

5 Place each decal in turn in a bowl of water and leave for 30 seconds until you can feel the backing paper starting to slide off.

6 Remove from the water with the backing paper still attached, and place it on your ceramic item. Smooth the decal down while gently sliding out the backing paper. Smooth over the decal with your finger to remove any air bubbles. Repeat with the remaining decals.

7 Preheat your oven to 130°C/250°F/Gas ½ and place your ceramic item on the middle shelf. Leave it there to dry for 10–15 minutes, then remove and leave to cool.

4

6

DOORSTOP CUBE

This cube doorstop is a great alternative to a traditional, solid doorstop. It is nice and soft but is filled with sand or rice to add weight and hold the door in place.

LEVEL:

PRINTING TECHNIQUE

Lino print

MATERIALS

Fabric: cut one, 8 x 51in (20 x 130cm)

Handle: cut two, 2 x 8in (5 x 20cm)

Strong plastic bag

Sand or rice, for filling

Scissors, pins, needle, matching thread

PRINTING TOOLS

Print motif on page 118

Lino sheet

Lino cutter

Craft knife

Fabric paint in 3 colors

Sponge

Sponge or sponge roller

1 This design is applied using the lino print technique on pages 12–13. Prepare your stamp using the motif on page 118. To print, load the stamp with fabric paint using a sponge or a sponge roller. Practice first on a scrap of fabric until you are confident you can achieve a clean, clear print that is correctly lined up.

2 Iron your fabric, cut it to size, and lay it on a flat surface ready for printing. Build up your design by printing in vertical rows. The top of each print should touch the bottom of the last print. After printing one row, rotate the lino stamp 180 degrees for the next row. Make sure the sides of the prints in the second row are touching the sides of the prints in the first row. You can change your colors when you like. I tried to build up a random pattern but you could use one color for each row.

2

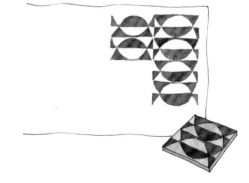

3 When you are happy with your finished design, iron the fabric to set the paint.

4 Now you must cut the strip into six 7 x 7in (18 x 18cm) squares. You will create the doorstop by sewing the squares together to form a cube. Choose one of your squares as the bottom of your doorstop. With right sides together, pin and sew four side panels around each side of the first square. Leave a ½in (1cm) seam allowance and start and end each seam ½in (1cm) from the corner. Lift up the four panels and, still with the wrong sides of the fabric facing you, sew them together to make a cube. You will sew the final square onto the top of the cube in step 6.

5 Next you need to make up your handle. With right side to right side, sew the two handle pieces together with a ½in (1cm) seam down both edges. Turn to the right side and press to get nice crisp edges. Topstitch a neat line of stitches close to both edges.

6 Now you need to attach the top panel and the handle at the same time. Pin the handle to the center of the top panel then, with right sides together, pin the sides of the top panel to the four side panels, sandwiching the ends of the handle between the layers. Sew around the sides of the top panel, leaving a ½in (1cm) seam allowance.

7 Turn the doorstop to the right side through the opening, then push out the corners from the inside to make sure the cube has a good shape.

8 Line the cube with a strong plastic bag so your filling doesn't escape through the seams, then use a funnel to fill the cube with sand or rice until the doorstop is firm.

9 Tie a tight knot in the plastic bag and tuck it inside the cube. Hand-sew the opening closed and your doorstop is ready to use.

PRINTING TIPS

This motif is printed in vertical rows. Rotate the lino stamp 180 degrees every other row to build up the pattern.

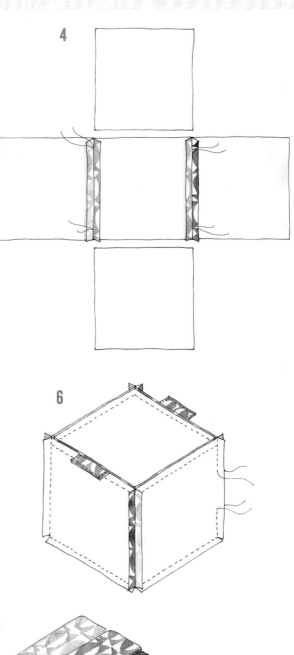

2 UNIQUE KITCHEN

FULL-LENGTH APRON

Every maker needs a stylish apron to protect their clothes and simply to look wonderful! Whether for your kitchen or your craft room, this easy-to-make fully-lined apron is perfect for your needs.

LEVEL: 🐦 🐦 🐦

PRINTING TECHNIQUE

Screen printing

MATERIALS

Fabric templates on pages 124–125

Main fabric:

Apron: cut one, 36 x 28in (90 x 70cm)

Pocket: cut one, 20 x 12in (50 x 30cm)

Lining fabric:

Apron: cut one, 36 x 28in (90 x 70cm)

Pocket: cut one, 20 x 12in (50 x 30cm)

Cotton tape: approx. 2 x 79in (5cm x 2m)

Tailor's chalk

Scissors, pins, needle, matching thread, tape measure

PRINTING TOOLS

Print motif on page 119

Letter-sized (A4) screen

Plain paper

Craft knife

Parcel tape

Fabric paint

Squeegee

1 This design is applied using the screen-printing technique on pages 14–15. Prepare your stencil using the leaf motif on page 119. Place the motif in the very center of your sheet of paper. The image should fit within the area of the mesh, make sure you leave a border of 4in (10cm) of blank paper around the image.

2 Turn your screen mesh-side up and place your paper stencil on top. Make sure the motif is in the center, then use parcel tape around the edges to attach it.

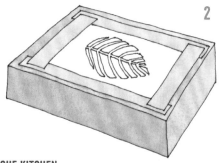

PRINTING TIPS

This is a great way to try out screen-printing and work with a large repeatable pattern. If you don't want to screen-print, you could just use this as a simple stencil and use a sponge to apply the paint.

5

6

3 Iron your fabrics and cut them to size, then cut them out using the templates on pages 124–125.

4 Once your screen and stencil are ready, practice on a scrap of fabric until you are confident you can achieve a clean, clear print. Lay your screen stencil side down on the apron fabric, put a generous blob of paint on the screen above the image, then drag the paint across the surface with even pressure using a squeegee. Drag the paint back and forth across the image two or three times. Your first pass of ink will secure the paper stencil in place to the mesh side of the screen. Carefully lift up the screen and reposition it for the next print.

5 Build up your design by printing the leaf motif randomly. Leave plenty of space between each leaf and rotate each one to add variety and interest. Remember to print a leaf on the pocket piece, too. Once the paint is dry, iron the fabric to set the paint.

6 To make up the apron, start with the pocket. With the main and lining fabric pieces right sides together, leave a ½in (1cm) seam allowance and sew all around the edges. Leave a small opening in the bottom edge for turning.

7 Trim the corners of the pocket and turn to the right side through the opening. Hand-sew the opening closed.

8 To attach the pocket to the front of the apron, use the template on page 125 and mark in chalk where the pocket should go. Pin the pocket in place, then sew a neat line of stitches around the sides and bottom edge to secure the pocket. Reverse-stitch a few times at the top corners of the pocket as this is where there will be the most stress. Sew a line of stitches down the center and through the apron to divide the pocket into two sections.

9 Now pin the neck strap and the ties made from the cotton tape in place. Cut the neck strap longer than you need, then you can adjust it with a knot once it is finished. Pin the ends of the neck strap to the top of the apron about 2in (5cm) from the corners, with the loop of the strap facing down. Cut the ties so they are long enough to go around you and tie at the back. Pin the ties to the sides of the apron about 2in (5cm) down from the corners and facing inward.

10 Place the lining on top of your main fabric, right sides together, and pin all around, making sure the strap and ties are tucked inside. Leaving a ½in (1cm) seam allowance, sew all around the edges. Leave a small opening in the bottom edge for turning.

11 Trim all the corners and clip the curves, taking care not to cut through the stitches (see page 115). Turn the apron to the right side through the opening, Push out all the corners and press the edges flat. Topstitch a neat line of stitches all the way around the apron, closing the opening at the bottom edge as you go.

TABLE RUNNER

This runner is an elegant addition to any table. It's a great way to bring in design and color without having to print the whole surface of a tablecloth. Measure your own table and adjust the size of the runner according to your needs.

LEVEL: 🐦 🐦

PRINTING TECHNIQUE

Screen-printing

MATERIALS

Fabric: 16 x 71in (40 x 180cm)

Scissors, matching thread

PRINTING TOOLS

Print motif on page 117

Embroidery hoop: 10in (26cm) and fine nylon mesh fabric or readymade screen-printing frame

Pencil

Screen filler

Paintbrush

Parcel tape

Hairdryer (optional)

Fabric paint in 2 colors

Old credit card or squeegee

1 This design is applied using the screen-printing technique on pages 14–15. If you are going to make your own screen from an embroidery hoop and nylon mesh, follow the instructions on page 15. If you have a readymade screen, move straight to step 2.

2 Prepare your design using the motif on page 117 and draw it directly onto the screen mesh in pencil. Make sure to leave a 2in (5cm) gap all around the edge of the motif.

3 Using the screen filler, carefully paint all the areas around your design with an even coat. Once this is dry, it will act as a barrier, stopping any fabric paint seeping through onto the fabric in those areas. You don't need to paint right to the edges of the screen, just up to 2in (5cm) all around the design. The edges will be covered with parcel tape in step 4.

4 Leave to dry for at least an hour—you can use a hairdryer to speed things up. Once the filler is completely dry, cover the edges of the screen with parcel tape so no paint can get through to the fabric in areas where it shouldn't. Make sure the tape comes up around the edges.

5 Now iron your fabric and cut it to size: the measurements given include ¾in (2cm) all around for the hems—adjust your measurements if you need to. Lay the fabric on a flat surface ready for printing. If you can't lay it out in one long line, print half the fabric first, then turn it around to print the other half. Practice first on a scrap of fabric until you are confident you can achieve a clean, clear print.

6 The pattern is built up in rows, with the darker color printed first and the lighter color overlaid afterward. Lay your screen mesh-side down where you want the first print to go. Add a generous blob of the darker fabric paint to the top of the screen, just above the design. Using the credit card or squeegee, scrape the paint across the surface of the screen in one steady action. Repeat a couple more times back and forth, then carefully lift up the screen. Dry your print with a hair dryer.

7 Continue printing your fabric in this way to build up your design. Let each print dry before moving the screen to its next position.

8 Once you have covered your fabric with prints in this color, wash your screen thoroughly under running water and leave to dry. Repeat steps 6 and 7 using your light paint color and staggering the prints to achieve an attractive effect, using the photo opposite as a guide. Make sure you wash your screen when you have finished and it will be usable for another project. When you are happy with your finished design, iron the fabric to set the paint.

9 Fold the raw edges of the runner to the wrong side by ½in (1cm), then fold them again by ½in (1cm). Press in place, then stitch neatly along the first fold. See page 115 for a clever way to finish the corners.

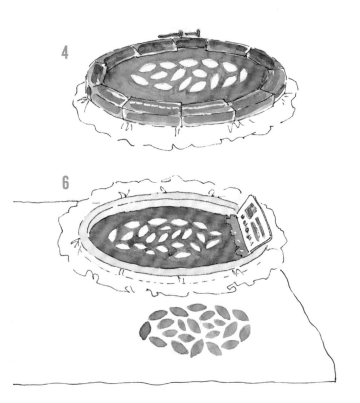

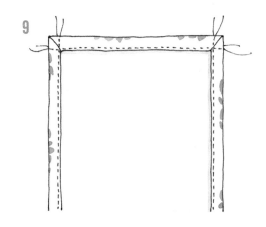

PRINTING TIPS

This is a simple screen-printing technique using painted-on filler to create your stencil. This project shows you how to make your own screen using familiar craftroom objects. You can use the same technique with a readymade screen, too.

QUILTED OVEN GLOVE

This oven glove not only gives practical protection when you're taking your baking out of the oven, but is a stylish addition to any kitchen. You could use colors that match your decor or add a bright splash of contrast color if you prefer.

LEVEL: 🐦 🐦

PRINTING TECHNIQUE

Fruit and vegetable print

MATERIALS

Fabric template on page 125

Main fabric:

Front and back: cut two, 8 x 13in (20 x 33cm)

Hanging loop: 4 x 2in (10 x 5cm)

Lining fabric: cut two, 8 x 13in (20 x 33cm)

Thermal wadding: cut two, 8 x 13in (20 x 33cm)

Matching thread

PRINTING TOOLS

Print motifs on page 117

2 potatoes

Kitchen knife

Pencil eraser

Fabric paint in 3 colors

Sponge

1. This design is applied using the fruit and vegetable printing technique on page 11. Carve your potatoes using the pairs of leaves and stems motifs on page 117. The berries are added afterward, using a pencil eraser as a stamp. Practice first on a scrap of fabric until you are confident you can achieve a clean, clear print.

2. Iron your fabric, cut it to size, and lay it on a flat surface ready for printing. First load the leaf stamp with fabric paint using a sponge.

3. Start at the bottom left-hand corner of the fabric and print the pairs of leaves in rows, staggering each row like a brick pattern. Then load the stems stamp with fabric paint in another color and add those between each pair of leaves. Finally load the pencil eraser with fabric paint in the third color to add the berries to the stems. Don't forget to print the piece of fabric for your hanging loop, too.

4. When you are happy with your finished design, iron the fabric to set the paint.

5. Cut out your printed fabric, lining, and wadding using the templates on page 125. Trim the wadding so it is ½in (1cm) smaller all around than the printed fabric.

PRINTING TIPS

This print is made up of three elements
layered one on top of the other. You start
by printing the pairs of big leaves, then
everything else will fit in. Practice your
placement on scrap fabric first till you
are confident. If you are really aiming at
perfection, mark your fabric with chalk lines
and follow these when you print.

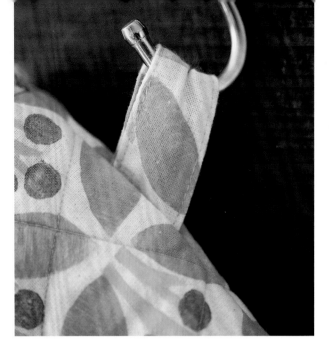

6 Now you are going to pad the printed fabric for heat protection. Do this by laying a piece of wadding on the wrong side of each piece of the printed fabric. Pin or tack the wadding in place so it won't move about.

7 Working on the right side of the printed fabric, machine-sew the two together using criss-crossed diagonal lines of stitching spaced approximately 1in (3cm) apart.

8 To create your hanging loop, press a narrow hem along both long edges of the loop fabric, then fold the fabric lengthwise, bringing the two folded edges together. Topstitch a neat line of stitches down each side of the loop fabric.

9 Place the two quilted pieces of fabric right sides together. Tuck the hanging loop between them, facing inward. Leaving a ½in (1cm) seam allowance, sew all around the edge, making sure to avoid catching the wadding in your stitches, as this will make the seam too bulky. Trim more wadding away if necessary.

10 Clip the curves and especially round the thumb, taking care not to cut through the stitches. Leave the glove inside out.

11 Now you are going to make up your lining. Place the two pieces of lining right sides together. Leaving a ½in (1cm) seam allowance, sew all around the edge. Clip the curves and the thumb, being careful not to cut through the stitches. Turn to the right side.

12 Insert the lining into the quilted glove so the right sides of both are facing. Line up the bottom edges, then sew around the bottom edge, leaving a ½in (1cm) seam allowance. Leave a 4in (10cm) opening. Pull the glove to the right side through the opening. Push all the curves and the thumb out fully. Tuck the lining back inside the glove, but leave a ½in (1cm) border of lining around the glove opening. Pin the opening closed. You will sew it closed in the next step.

13 Tuck your glove over the free arm of your sewing machine and sew a ½in (1cm) seam along the edge of the lining.

7
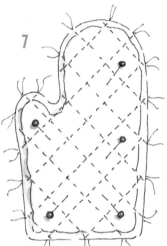

9
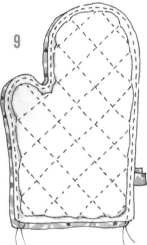

13

CAFETIÈRE COZY

This is a smart way to keep
your coffee warm for hours.
Thick industrial felt is
available from felt specialists
online and you can buy small
sheets, which are perfect for
a few craft projects like
this one.

LEVEL: 🐦

PRINTING TECHNIQUE

Household item print

MATERIALS

¼in (5mm) thick felt: 16 x 7in (40 x 18cm)

Leather strip or ribbon: ¼ x 20in (6mm x 50cm)

Paper

Scissors

Craft knife

PRINTING TOOLS

Wooden block: approx. 2½ x 1in (6 x 2.5cm)

Masking tape

Thin string or garden twine

Sponge

Fabric paint

1 Measure the height and circumference of the glass part of your cafetière and cut out a paper pattern that will wrap around the cafetière and overlap slightly. Cut out your felt so it is a little larger than the pattern. It's hard to print neatly over the edge of a piece of fabric: it's far simpler to print first, then cut to size afterward. Lay your felt on a flat surface ready for printing. My suggested measurements should fit most eight-cup cafetières.

2 The design is applied using the household item print technique on page 11. To make your printing block, use masking tape to attach one end of a piece of thin string or garden twine to one wide face of your block. Wrap the string tightly around the block till it is covered with a web of string, then attach the other end of the string to the face of the block where you started. You now have a printing block.

3 Use a sponge to coat the string lightly with fabric paint on the wide face of the block that is free of masking tape. Practice first on a scrap of fabric until you are confident you can achieve a clean, clear print.

PRINTING TIPS

This print is made with a wooden block wrapped in string that's used to make a simple herringbone pattern. You can vary the angles of your lines, as well as how far apart they are spaced—experiment with the pattern to get a different result each time.

4 Make your first print in the center of the fabric on a diagonal and build up the herringbone pattern from there, turning the printing block through 90 degrees after each print.

5 Once you've covered the whole of the felt, iron it on a low heat to set the paint.

6 Now you can cut out the cozy shape using the paper pattern. To form the overlapping tab that will keep your cozy closed, use a craft knife or scissors to cut away two rectangles from one short side, leaving a tab in the middle that is approximately 1½in (4cm) deep by 3in (8cm) high.

7 Cut 2 vertical slits in the tab approximately ¾in (2cm) apart. Cut two matching slits along the other short side, approximately ½in (4cm) from the edge.

8 Thread your leather strip or ribbon from the wrong side of the felt through the slits on the side of the cozy without the tab. Wrap the cozy around the cafetière, thread the leather strip or ribbon through the slits in the tab and tie the cozy closed.

4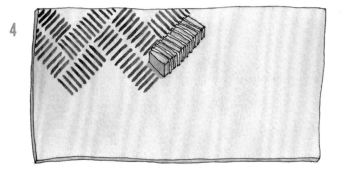

6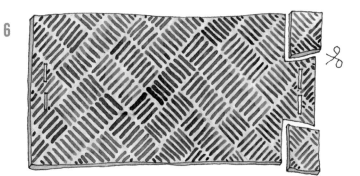

8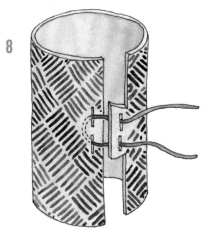

BIRD-PRINT TEA TOWEL

A tea towel can be both useful and beautiful in your kitchen. Use a strong cotton or linen fabric so it's up to the job of drying all your pots and pans. It's such a simple and easy project, you can make a few so you always have a clean one ready to use. They also make great housewarming gifts, so make one for all your friends, too.

LEVEL:

PRINTING TECHNIQUE

Stencil

MATERIALS

Fabric: 15 x 22in (38 x 55cm)

Cotton tape: 1 x 4in (2.5 x 10cm)

Tailor's chalk

Pins, matching thread, black thread

PRINTING TOOLS

Print motifs on page 119

Craft knife

Freezer paper or plain paper

Temporary spray adhesive (optional)

Sponge

Fabric paint

Hairdryer (optional)

1 Iron your fabric, cut it to size and lay it on a flat surface. Mark in tailor's chalk where you want the "wires" to be placed.

2 The design is applied using the stencil technique on page 14. Prepare your stencils using the three different bird motifs on page 119.

3 Place each stencil in turn in your chosen position along the chalk line. If your stencil is made from freezer paper, you can iron it in place, otherwise lightly spray the back with temporary spray adhesive.

4 Sponge the fabric paint onto the fabric through the stencil. Practice first on a scrap of fabric until you are confident you can achieve a clean, clear print. Once the paint is dry—you can use a hairdryer to speed up the process—peel the stencil away very carefully, then move on to the next bird. When you are happy with your finished design, iron the fabric to set the paint.

5 Now finish off the design by machine-stitching the black wires for the birds to sit on.

6 The last step is to hem the raw edges of the tea towel. With the wrong side facing you, fold under the raw edges along all four sides and pin. Fold the fabric under a second time, this time by ½in (1cm), so the raw edges are enclosed. Press the folds flat.

7 Before you sew, make the hanging loop by tucking your piece of cotton tape under the adjacent hems in the top left-hand corner of the tea towel. Now sew a neat line of stitches close to the edge of the first fold to keep everything in place. Secure the ends of the tape in your stitching as you go and take care to stitch a neat right angle around the corners.

PRINTING TIPS

This design is created using stencils for the birds and lines of stitching for the wires. Print your birds in small groups along the "wires" to balance the design.

4

5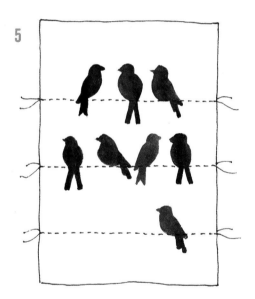

7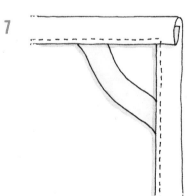

VINE-LEAF PLACEMAT

This placemat doesn't involve any sewing—just some clever cutting and an elegant wreath design.

LEVEL:

PRINTING TECHNIQUE

Stencil

MATERIALS

Fabric template on page 124

Felt: 16 x 14in (40 x 35cm), per placemat

Chalk pencil

Large and small scissors

PRINTING TOOLS

Print motif on page 121

Craft knife

Freezer paper or plain paper

Temporary spray adhesive (optional)

Sponge

Fabric paint

PRINTING TIPS

This is a very delicate stencil, so take great care when cutting it out and ironing it on to the felt.

1 Cut your felt to size and lay it on a flat surface. Cut the decorative edge along one short side before you do any printing. Using the fabric template on page 124 and a chalk pencil, draw the edging design onto the felt. Cut it out with a small pair of sharp scissors.

2 The design is applied using the stencil technique on page 14. Prepare your stencil using the wreath motif on page 121.

3 Place the stencil in the center of your piece of felt. If your stencil is made from freezer paper, you can iron it in place (use a low heat setting to avoid shrinking the felt), otherwise lightly spray the back with temporary spray adhesive.

4 Sponge the fabric paint onto the felt through the stencil. Practice first on a scrap of fabric until you are confident you can achieve a clean, clear print.

5 Once the paint is dry, peel the stencil away very carefully. Iron on a low heat to set the fabric paint.

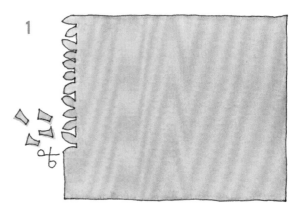

LEAF-FALL NAPKIN

Napkins can transform a dinner table. You can theme them according to the season or you can personalize them for your guests. They are also a great way to use up pieces of fabric from your stash.

1 This design is applied using the eraser stamp technique on page 12. Prepare your stamps using the leaf motifs on page 117. Iron your fabric, cut it to size, and lay it on a flat surface ready for printing.

2 Load each stamp with fabric paint using a sponge, and build up your design on the fabric, printing one leaf at a time. Practice first on a scrap of fabric until you are confident you can achieve a clean, clear print.

3 When you are happy with your design, iron the fabric to set the paint.

4 Once your fabric is ready, with the wrong side facing you, fold under the raw edges along all four sides and pin. Fold the fabric under a second time, this time by ½in (1cm), so the raw edge is enclosed. Press the folds flat then sew a neat line of stitches close to the edge of the first fold to keep everything in place. Take care to stitch a neat right angle around the corners. Trim the threads and you're done.

5 The whole thing is so easy, you're sure to want to make a set of four, six, or even eight.

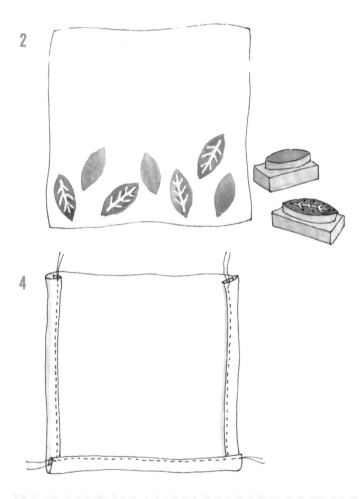

PRINTING TIPS

The two simple leaf motifs allow you to build up any design you want. Have a play on some scrap fabric first to help you work out the perfect design for your needs.

PRINTING TECHNIQUE

Eraser stamp

MATERIALS

Fabric: 14 x 14in (35 x 35cm), per napkin

Scissors

Pins, matching thread

PRINTING TOOLS

Print motifs on page 117

2 large erasers

Wooden or acrylic backing block

Glue

Lino cutter

Craft knife

Fabric paint

Sponge

FERN-PRINT COASTERS

This no-sew project is a simple introduction to screen-printing. Coasters are always useful to protect your precious surfaces, especially if you make them from thick felt. They are a great housewarming gift and can be made to any shape or size. This project makes four coasters, cut into simple circles. It's easier to print the entire piece of felt, then cut the circles out afterward.

LEVEL:

PRINTING TECHNIQUE

Screen-printing

MATERIALS

Thick felt: 12 x 12in (30 x 30cm)

Fine nylon mesh: 15 x 15in (38 x 38cm)

Paper

Pair of compasses

Scissors

Tailor's chalk

PRINTING TOOLS

Print motif on page 119

Embroidery hoop: 10in (26cm)

Pencil

Screen drawing fluid

Paintbrush

Hairdryer

Screen filler

Old credit card or squeegee

Parcel tape

Fabric paint

1 This design is applied using the screen-printing technique on pages 14–15. If you are going to make your own screen, follow the instructions on page 16. If you have a readymade screen, move straight to step 2.

2 You need to transfer the fern motif from page 119 onto your screen. Place the screen mesh-side down, on the photocopied and enlarged motif. Trace over the motif in pencil directly onto the mesh. Make sure to leave a 2in (5cm) gap all around the edge of the motif.

3 Now, with your screen mesh-side up, you can paint on the motif using the blue-colored screen drawing fluid and a paintbrush. The fluid has a runny PVA-type consistency. You need to achieve a good solid line—if it's too thin, your printing won't work. Remember, practice makes perfect. Leave the mesh to dry fully; you can use a hairdryer on a low heat if necessary.

3

4 Once your design is dry, you must coat your screen with
screen filler. Do this with an old credit card or squeegee. Pour
a blob of screen filler on the card and drag it across the screen,
covering the surface with a thin, even coat of filler. Take care not
to overdo this or the drawing fluid will start to dissolve. Just drag
the card quickly and smoothly once or twice across the screen.
You don't need to go right to the edges of the screen as these
will be covered with parcel tape later on. Leave to dry completely,
using a hairdryer on a low heat to speed things up.

5 Once the filler is completely dry, wash out the drawing fluid
under running water. Allow the water to run over both sides of
the screen and after a few seconds you should see the drawing
fluid start to disappear. You may need to rub gently in some areas
but be careful, as too much rubbing will ruin the screen.

6 Hold the screen up to the light to check the drawing fluid has
completely vanished. The edges of your design should be
clearly defined and clear, both of drawing fluid and of filler. Leave
the screen to dry.

7 Now prepare your screen for printing by covering the edges
with parcel tape so no ink can get through to the fabric in
areas where it shouldn't.

8 To print your felt, lay it flat. Place your screen mesh-side
down, on one corner of the felt. Put a generous blob of fabric
paint on top and, using the credit card or squeegee, scrape the
paint across the surface of the screen in one steady action.
Repeat a couple more times, then carefully lift up the screen. If
you've used too much paint or too much pressure, there will be
bleeds of paint on your felt. If you haven't used enough paint or
enough pressure, your print will be incomplete. Practice first on a
scrap of fabric until you are confident you can achieve a clean,
clear print.

9 Work your way across the felt to build up the design.

PRINTING TIPS

This is a simple homemade screen-
printing technique. You can make your
own screen out of an embroidery hoop
and nylon mesh or use a readymade
screen (see page 16 for more details).
Practice lining up the repeat on scrap
fabric before you print the felt.

5

8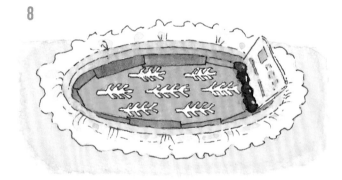

10 As soon as you have covered the felt, wash your screen. Leave the paint to dry, then iron on a low heat to set it.

11 Make a paper template 4in (10cm) in diameter, using a pair of compasses, set to 2in (5cm). Cut out the template, lay it on the printed felt and draw around it with tailor's chalk. Cut the felt out carefully. Repeat until you've cut out all four of your coasters.

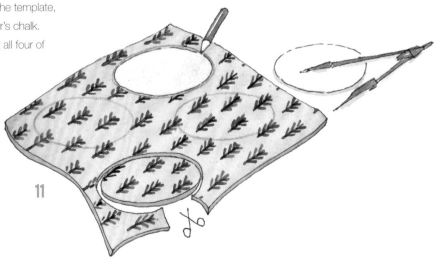

11

TEA COZY

A timeless classic, this project shows you how to make your own quilted tea cozy to keep a refreshing pot of tea warm for ages. This tea cozy will fit a teapot that is 6in (15cm) tall and 12in (30cm) wide, but you can adapt it to fit your own teapot by measuring your teapot and making the template larger or smaller.

PRINTING TECHNIQUE

Foam stamp

MATERIALS

Fabric template on page 126

Main fabric:

Panel 1: cut two, 10 x 12in (25 x 30cm)

Panel 2: cut two, 5 x 12in (12 x 30cm)

Panel 3: cut two, 5 x 12in (12 x 30cm)

Teabag tag: cut two, 2½ x 2½in (6 x 6cm)

Lining fabric: cut two, 17¾ x 12in (45 x 30cm)

Wadding: cut two, 17¾ x 12in (45 x 30cm)

Short length of ribbon

Needle, pins, matching thread

PRINTING TOOLS

Print motifs on page 121

Foam sheets

Scissors

Wooden or acrylic backing block

Glue

Pencil eraser

Fabric paint

Sponge or sponge roller

1 This tea cozy is made up of three printed panels joined together to make one piece of fabric for each side of the tea cosy.

2 The design is applied using the foam stamp technique on page 13. Prepare your foam stamps using the teapot and teacup motifs on page 121.

3 Iron your fabrics and cut them to size, making them a little larger than the fabric template requires. Lay the fabrics on a flat surface for printing.

4 Load your teapot stamp with fabric paint using a sponge and apply to each of the two large panels of fabric, one for each side of the cozy. Practice first on a scrap of fabric until you are confident you can achieve a clean, clear print.

5 Now load a pencil eraser with fabric paint using a sponge, then use this to build up the spots around the teapots. You might like to leave some areas of fabric unprinted, as I've done. Build up the spots in the same way on both sets of the smaller panels of fabric.

6 To make the little teabag tag, cut the fabric to the size required and print a teacup centrally on each piece. Iron all your printed fabrics to set the paint.

7 Now you must join the three panels of printed fabric together for each side of the cozy. Join one panel to the next, right side to right side and sew them together leaving a ½in (1cm) seam allowance. Repeat until you have two lots of three panels.

8 Press the seams open and topstitch neatly down both sides of each seam, as a decorative detail.

9 Now you are going to use the fabric template on page 126 to cut each set of panels into the shape of the tea cozy. Use the template to shape your two pieces of lining fabric and the two pieces of wadding as well.

7

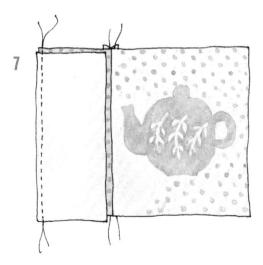

10 Quilting the lining fabric will make the tea cosy hold the heat better. Do this by laying a piece of wadding on the wrong side of each piece of lining fabric, then sew the two together using criss-crossed diagonal lines of stitching spaced approximately 2in (5cm) apart.

11 You now have two quilted pieces of lining. With right side to right side and leaving a ½in (1cm) seam allowance, sew them together around the curved edge to make a quilted lining pouch.

12 You now need to make the little teabag tag. Lay your two pieces of printed teabag fabric with right sides together, making sure the teacup print is the same way up on each side. Pin the ends of your ribbon in between at the center top (the rim of the printed teacup), with the loop facing inward.

13 Leaving a ½in (1cm) seam allowance, sew around all four sides of the tag. Leave a small opening for turning. Trim the corners, turn right side out and press. Pin the opening closed and sew a neat line of topstitches all around the edge.

14 Now line up the two shaped pieces of printed fabric with right sides together and pin the ribbon ends of your teabag tag in between the two layers at the center top. Leaving a ½in (1cm) seam allowance, sew around the curved edge, then clip the curves, taking care not to cut through the stitches. Turn right side out and press.

15 To construct your tea cozy, insert the printed fabric into the lining fabric pouch with right sides together. Pin together all around the bottom edge. Leaving a ½in (1cm) seam allowance, sew around the bottom edge, leaving a small opening for turning.

16 Turn to the right side through the opening, push the lining inside, and handsew the opening closed to finish your tea cozy.

PRINTING TIPS

To give this project a twist, I printed two different types of fabric and joined them before cutting out the shape of the tea cozy. You can create the spotty pattern by building up the spots with a stamp made from a pencil eraser.

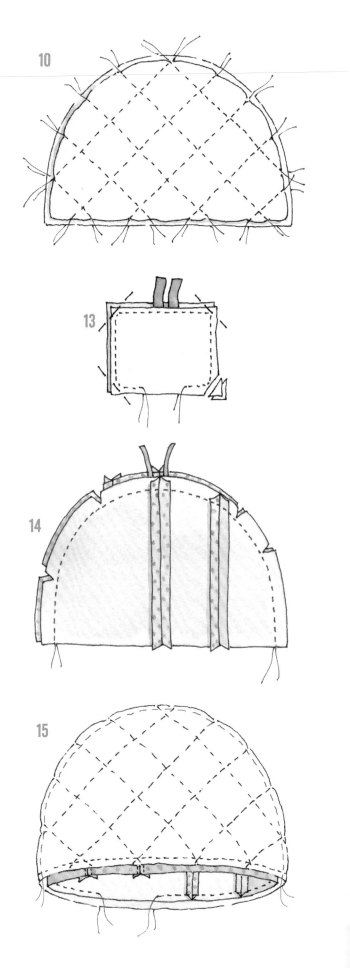

FEATHER-PRINT POT HOLDER

A useful little addition to your kitchen, this is great for holding hot pot handles or for resting a hot pot on. It's perfectly padded to protect your hands and surfaces.

LEVEL: 🐦

PRINTING TECHNIQUE

Foam stamp

MATERIALS

Fabric:

Front and back: cut two, 9 x 9in (22 x 22cm)

Hanging loop: 4 x 2in (10 x 5cm)

Thermal wadding: 8 x 8in (20 x 20cm)

Pins, matching thread

PRINTING TOOLS

Print motifs on page 118

Foam sheets

Craft knife

Scissors

Acrylic backing block

Glue

Fabric paint

Sponge

1 This design is applied using the foam stamp technique on page 13. Prepare your stamp using the arrow feathers motif on page 118. Use an acrylic block as a backing block if you can, to make it easier to line up your prints.

2 Iron your fabric, cut two pieces measuring 9 x 9in (22 x 22cm), and lay them on a flat surface ready for printing.

3 Load the stamp with fabric paint using a sponge. Practice first on a scrap of fabric until you are confident you can achieve a clean, clear print.

4 Now start printing in one corner of the fabric and build up your design working in diagonal rows. Take care to join up the arrow feathers neatly and rotate the stamp every other row. When you are happy with your finished design, iron the two pieces of fabric to set the paint.

5 Cut your piece of thermal wadding to size, so that it measures 8 x 8in (20 x 20cm).

6 To make sure the wadding doesn't move about, tack it roughly with large, loose stitches to the wrong side of one of the printed fabric pieces.

7 Now make the hanging loop. Cut the fabric to size and fold over a very narrow hem down both long sides. Press to form two neat edges, then fold the fabric lengthwise to bring the edges together. Sew a neat line of stiches down both edges.

4

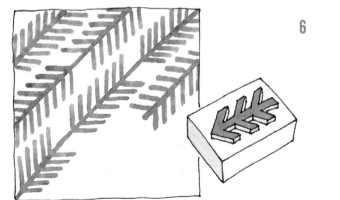

6

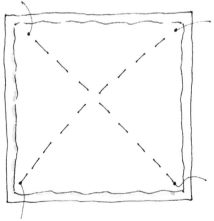

8 Next you are going to join all the pieces together. Lay the printed pieces of fabric with right sides facing. Match up their edges and pin. Fold the hanging loop and tuck it, loop facing inward, between the two pieces of printed fabric.

9 Sew around all four sides leaving a ½in (1cm) seam allowance. Secure the hanging loop in your stitching as you go. Leave a small opening along one side for turning.

10 Turn the whole pot holder to the right side through the opening, making sure the wadding is lying flat inside. Pin the opening closed, then sew a neat line of topstitching close to the edge to finish. For extra detail I have done two rows of topstitching.

11 To create the quilted effect, sew crisscrossed diagonal lines of stitching spaced approximately 1in (3cm) apart over the whole of the pan holder.

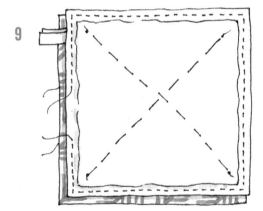

9

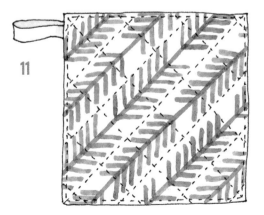

11

PRINTING TIPS
Using an acrylic backing block for your foam stamp will make it easier for you to line up your repeat print correctly.

SQUARE ENVELOPE CUSHION COVER

This quick and easy stencil idea works brilliantly to spice up a cushion cover. I've made an envelope cover. It's easy as there are no zips to fit! This project will make a cushion cover that will fit an 18in (46cm) cushion pad but you can adapt the size if you want a bigger or a smaller one.

LEVEL: 🐦

PRINTING TECHNIQUE

Masking tape stencil

MATERIALS

Fabric:

Front piece: cut one, 19 x 19in (48 x 48cm)

Back pieces: cut two, 19 x 14in (48 x 35cm)

Cushion pad: 18 x 18in (46 x 46cm)

Scissors, pins, matching thread

PRINTING TOOLS

Masking tape

Sponge

Fabric paint in three colors

Hairdryer

1 This design is applied using the masking tape stencil technique on page 14. Iron your fabric, cut it to size and lay your front piece on a flat surface ready for printing. You are going to use masking tape to make the triangle shapes and you will print one triangle at a time. Practice first on a scrap of fabric until you are confident you can achieve a clean, clear print.

2 Mask along the edges of the largest triangle first and sponge on your paint, working from the point of the triangle downward. Sponge the paint on more heavily at the point and more lightly as you move down. Use a hairdryer to dry the paint, then remove the tape.

3 Mask off your next triangle so it overlaps the first, then sponge on another color paint in the same way. Repeat until you have a design you are happy with, then finish by ironing your fabric to set the paint.

4 Cut out the two back pieces. With the wrong side of one back piece facing you, fold under the raw edge along one long side and pin. Fold the fabric under a second time, this time by 1½in (4cm), so the raw edge is enclosed. Press the folds flat, then sew a neat line of stitches along the first fold to keep everything in place. Repeat for the second back piece.

5 Now you are going to bring all three pieces together to make the cushion cover. Lay the front piece down right side up and place one back piece on top, right side down with its unfolded edge on the top edge of the front piece. Now lay the other back piece on top with its unfolded edge on the bottom edge of the front piece. The two back pieces should overlap in the middle. Pin all the pieces in place. Leaving a ½in (1cm) seam allowance, sew along all four sides. Go carefully where the back pieces overlap as the layers will be very thick and harder to sew through. Trim away the four corners, taking care not to cut through the stitching, then turn the cushion cover right side out and press.

6 Insert your cushion pad through the opening and you're done.

PRINTING TIPS

I have used masking tape to create the shapes and have sponged on the paint heavily at the top of the triangles and lightly at the bottom to give different tones. You could create many different looks this way, get creative!

BOLSTER CUSHION

Bolster cushions come in many different sizes. They are great for neck support or to use on a bench or a window seat. This pattern introduces you to making a neat piped edge.

PRINTING TECHNIQUE

Lino stamp and eraser stamp

MATERIALS

Fabric:

Body: cut one (see instructions)

End pieces: cut two (see instructions)

Strips for piping cord: cut two
(see instructions)

Piping cord: cut two (see instructions)

Bolster cushion pad

Paper

Pair of compasses

Pencil

Scissors, needle, matching thread, zipper
foot, tape measure

PRINTING TOOLS

Print motif on page 121

Lino sheet

Large eraser

Lino cutter

Craft knife

Fabric paint in 3 colors

Sponge

1 The design is applied using the lino stamp and eraser stamp techniques on pages 12–13. Prepare your lino stamp using the seedhead motif on page 121 and make a simple circular eraser stamp about the same size as the lino stamp motif (see photo opposite for guidance). This will be used for the first layer of your design.

2 To print, load each stamp with one of the fabric paints using a sponge. Practice first on a scrap of fabric to help you decide what placement you like and to get the combination of colors just the way you want them

3 You will need to make a paper pattern for cutting out the fabric for the bolster. Measure the length of your bolster cushion and the circumference and diameter of the ends. Use a pair of compasses set to half the diameter of the end plus ½in (1cm) for your seam allowances, and draw two circles on paper.

4 Draw a large rectangle for the body, with its length the same as the length of the cushion plus 1in (2.5cm) for your seam allowances, and with its width equaling the circumference of the end, plus 1in (2.5cm) for your seam allowance.

5 Cut out the fabric for the body a bit larger than the pattern requires and cut large squares for the end pieces. Iron the fabric pieces and lay them on a flat surface ready for printing. You will cut the fabric to the exact pattern after printing.

6 First use the eraser stamp to print the fabric with circles. Leave to dry then use the lino stamp to overprint every other circle with the seedhead motif. Leave to dry again, then iron the fabric to set the paint. Don't forget to print the end pieces as well.

6

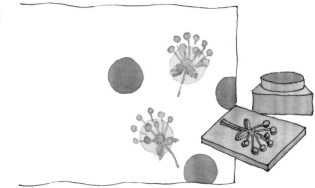

PRINTING TIPS

This is a two-layered print. You print the simple circles first, then overlay them with the seedhead motif using a lino stamp.

7 Now cut out the final fabric shapes using your paper pattern.

8 To start constructing your cushion, first you need to cover your piping cord. Cut two strips of fabric, each 4inch (10cm) longer than the circumference of the ends. Fold the fabric around the cord and, using your machine's zipper foot, sew as close to the cord as you can, enclosing the cord in the fabric. Trim the edge of the fabric to ⅜in (7mm).

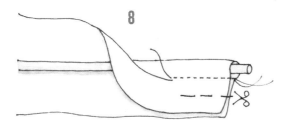

9 Now you need to attach the piping to the circular end pieces. Working on the right side of the fabric, line up the trimmed edge of the fabric-covered piping with the edge of an end piece. Still using your zipper foot, sew the piping to the end piece, stopping your stitching 2in (5cm) before the end.

10 To join the ends of the piping, peel back the fabric covering from the end of the piping and trim the piping cord so it meets the other end of the piping cord. Fold over the end of the fabric covering, then continue your line of machine stitching to complete the circle and secure the piping all around.

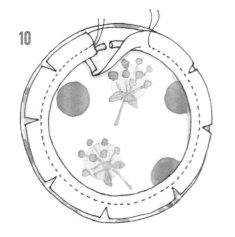

11 Once you have attached the piping to both end pieces, you can sew up the body to make a cylinder. With right sides together, fold the body lengthwise. Using a ½in (1cm) seam allowance, sew the two edges together, leaving a small opening in the center for turning.

12 Attach the circular end pieces by lining them up with the ends of the cylinder, right sides together. Still using your zipper foot, stitch the end pieces to the cylinder, following the line of stitching of the piping strip.

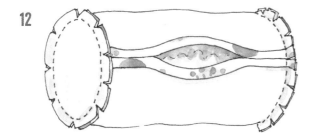

13 Turn your cover to the right side through the opening and insert the bolster cushion. Hand-sew the opening closed.

GIANT FLOOR CUSHIONS

These square cushions are great for providing extra comfy seating. You can stack them high and always have a spare for an unexpected guest.

PRINTING TECHNIQUE

Stencil

MATERIALS

Large cushion:

Fabric: 54 x 28½in (142 x 72cm)

Zipper: 30in (76cm)

Foam cushion pad: 20 x 20 x 6in (50 x 50 x 15cm) or polyester stuffing

Small cushion:

Fabric: 40 x 20.5in (102 x 52cm)

Zipper: 22in (55cm)

Foam cushion pad: 15 x 15 x 6in (38 x 38 x15cm) or polyester stuffing

Tailor's chalk

Scissors, pins, zipper foot, matching thread

PRINTING TOOLS

Print motif on page 120

Freezer paper or plain paper

Craft knife

Temporary spray adhesive (optional)

Sponge roller

Fabric paint

Hairdryer

1 This design is applied using the stencil technique on page 14. Prepare your stencil using the motif on page 120. Print out the motif and trace it onto freezer paper or plain paper. Repeat the motif across the whole piece of paper, then use a craft knife to cut out the shapes.

2 Iron your fabric, cut it to size and lay it on a flat surface ready for printing.

3 Place the stencil in one corner of the fabric. If your stencil is made from freezer paper, you can iron it in place, otherwise lightly spray the back with temporary spray adhesive.

4 Use the roller to sponge the fabric paint onto the fabric through the stencil. Practice first on a scrap of fabric until you are confident you can achieve a clean, clear print.

4

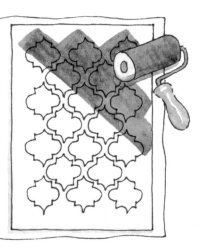

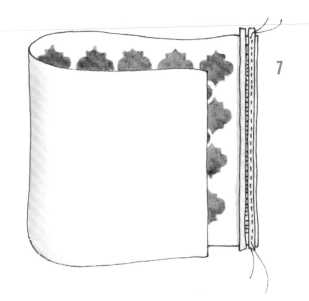

5 Use a hairdryer to dry the paint, then peel the stencil away from the fabric and reposition it, lining it up to the already-printed area to continue the design seamlessly. When you are happy with your finished design and all the fabric has been printed, iron the fabric to set the paint.

6 To make the cushion cover, you first need to attach the zipper to the short edge of the fabric. Lay your closed zipper face down on the right side of the fabric along one short edge. Using your zipper foot, sew the right edge of the zipper in place with a line of stitches close to the teeth. Fold over the other short edge of the fabric and line up the edge with the other side of the zipper. Sew this side of the zipper in the same way.

7 Turn the fabric to the right side and press the zipper seams flat to get a nice finish. Turn the cushion cover inside out again to complete the rest of the cushion.

8 Leaving a ½in (1cm) seam allowance, sew the long edges (the side seams) closed.

9 Next you need to give your cushion cover its boxy shape. Working on the wrong side, fold the fabric so that the seam with the zipper is flattened, the zipper is in the center, and two protruding corner triangles are created. For both sizes of cushion, measure 3in (7.5cm) from the point of each triangle and mark with tailor's chalk. From this point measure and mark two vertical lines 6in (15cm) long. These will be your stitch lines. Pin the corners in place. Repeat for the other two corners, then sew along your four stitch lines.

10 Turn your cushion cover to the right side and insert a foam cushion pad through the open zipper or stuff with polyester stuffing.

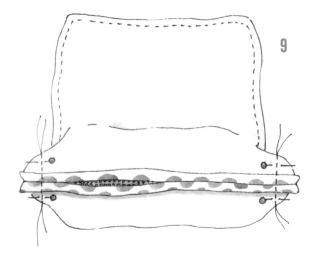

STYLISH COT BUMPER

Every new parent wants to keep their little one safe and warm inside their cot. This funky but practical cot bumper will do just that.

LEVEL: 🐦 🐦

PRINTING TECHNIQUE

Foam stamp

MATERIALS

Main fabric: cut six panels, 13.5 x 25in (34 x 64cm)

Wadding: cut three, 12.5 x 24.5in (32 x 62cm)

Ribbon: cut sixteen, 10 x ½in (26 x 1cm)

Pins, matching thread, tape measure

PRINTING TOOLS

Print motifs on page 120

2 foam sheets

Craft knife

Scissors

2 wooden or acrylic backing blocks

Glue

Fabric paint in 2 colors

Sponge

1 This design is applied using the foam stamp technique on page 13. Prepare your stamps using the paper crane motifs on page 120. To print, load the stamp with fabric paint using a sponge. Practice first on a scrap of fabric until you are confident you can achieve a clean, clear print.

2 Iron your main fabric, cut the six panels to size and lay them on a flat surface ready for printing. Start by printing one motif in diagonal lines across the fabric, leaving plenty of space between the motifs for the other motif. Leave to dry, then print the second motif in your second color between the first prints.

3 Print all six pieces of fabric. When you are happy with your finished design, iron the fabric to set the paint.

4 To construct the cot bumper, sew three of the printed panels together along their short edges, leaving a ½in (1cm) seam allowance. Make sure the printed motifs are all facing the same way up. This gives you one long, three-paneled strip of fabric. Repeat with the other three printed panels. You now have the front and back faces of the bumper.

5 Next you need to tack the wadding in place. With the wrong side of one strip facing you, lay a piece of wadding in the center of each panel and tack it in place with large, rough stitches to stop the wadding moving around.

6 Now pin two ribbons, facing inward, to the right side of the fabric at all four corners of the center panel and at each end of the entire strip.

7 Place the two long strips together, right side to right side and sew them together, leaving a ½in (1cm) seam allowance. Make sure to secure the ribbons in place as you sew. Leave a small opening in the bottom edge for turning. Remove the tacking stitches holding the wadding in place.

8 Trim the corners and turn to the right side through the opening, making sure that the wadding stays in place. Push out the corners and check that all the ribbons are secure. Press the edges of the bumper flat and straight and pin the opening closed.

9 Topstitch a neat line of stitches all the way around the bumper, closing the opening at the bottom edge as you go. Take care not to trap any ribbons in your topstitching.

10 To add the quilting, measure and mark with pins roughly every 4in (10cm) along the long edges of the bumper, then join the pins with lines of stitching through all the layers. You don't need to sew where the panels join. Once you have sewn about eight lines, you will need to turn your quilt and work from the other end, otherwise it becomes too bulky to manage.

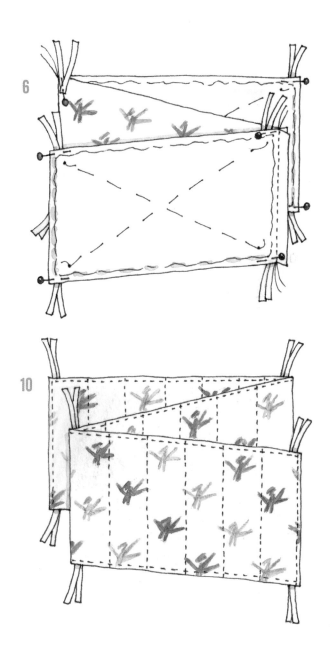

PRINTING TIPS

This design uses two different-sized motifs, printed alternately along diagonal lines. You can space out your design by eye, or measure and mark where you want your prints to go.

SIMPLE ROUND CUSHION

This lovely vintage-inspired cushion shape is so easy to make and adds a bit of timeless class to any chair. It consists of nothing more than two circles of fabric and a couple of buttons. You can, of course, adapt the size to suit your needs.

LEVEL: 🐦

PRINTING TECHNIQUE

Stencil

MATERIALS

Fabric: cut two, 20 x 20in (50 x 50cm), plus a scrap for covering button

2 buttons, at least 1in (25mm) diameter

Cushion filling or filling recycled from an old cushion

Sheet of paper

Pair of compasses (optional)

Scissors

Needle, pins, matching thread

PRINTING TOOLS

Print motifs on page 122

Freezer paper or plain paper

Craft knife

Temporary spray adhesive (optional)

Fabric paint in two colors

Sponge

Hairdryer

1 Iron your fabric and cut out your fabric squares to size. You will cut them into circles once you've printed the top of the cushion.

2 The overlapping flower print is applied using the stencil technique on page 14. Prepare your two-part stencil using the flower motifs on page 122.

3 You are only going to print one of the fabric squares. Lay it on a flat surface. You can start printing anywhere on the square. Position the first stencil on the fabric. If your stencil is made from freezer paper, you can iron it in place, otherwise lightly spray the back with temporary spray adhesive.

4 Sponge on the paint from the outer edge of the stencil in toward the middle so the center of the flower is as lightly colored as possible and the edges are bolder, using the photo on the right as a guide.

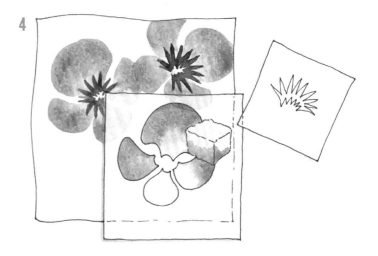

PRINTING TIPS

This print is built up using two stencils and two colors. The first stencil gives the bottom layer of petals and the second stencil provides the darker details. I made the pattern by randomly overlapping each flower, leaving unprinted fabric peeking through in just a few places. Washing the fabric after printing and heat-setting the paint stops the fabric from feeing heavy and stiff.

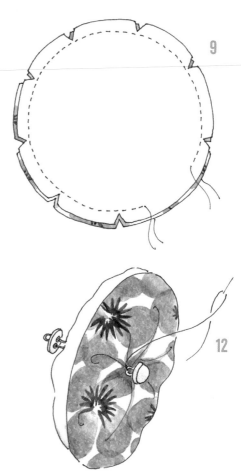

5 Use a hairdryer to dry the paint, then remove the stencil. Place the second stencil in place over your stenciled flower, keep it in place as before, then sponge on the darker paint, again sponging from the edge toward the center. Dry the paint and remove the stencil. Practice first on a scrap of fabric until you are confident you can achieve a clean, clear print with the two stencils.

6 Place your next flower so it slightly overlaps the first one. Position each stencil and sponge on the paint as before. Repeat until you have covered the fabric with printed flowers.

7 When you are happy with your design, iron the fabric to set the paint, then wash the fabric. Once it is dry, iron it again, ready to cut the pattern out.

8 Now you are ready to cut the fabric into circles with a diameter of 16in (40cm). Either use a pair of compasses set to 8in (20cm) to draw a circle on a piece of paper, or draw around an object that is 16in (40cm) diameter. Place your paper circle on top of each fabric square, pin it in place, and cut around it.

9 Place the two fabric circles together, right side to right side and pin. Leaving a ½in (1cm) seam allowance, sew around the edge. Leave a small opening for turning and stuffing. Clip at intervals along the seam, taking care not to cut through the stitches.

10 Turn to the right side through the opening, then stuff your cushion to the desired firmness with cushion filling. Handsew the opening closed, then plump up the cushion so the filling is even.

11 You can use any buttons for the center but I have used a fabric-covered button for the front and a plain button for the back. See page 116 to find out how to cover a button.

12 Find and mark the center of both sides of the cushion. Using a large needle, sew your covered button to the printed side at the center, then take the needle to the center back of the cushion and attach a second button there. Pull the thread tightly through both buttons and through all the layers of fabric, and lovely pleats will form.

OMBRE BEDLINEN

This is a great project for non-sewers. You start with plain white bedlinen and transform it using a dip-dyeing technique and stamps.

LEVEL: 🐦

PRINTING TECHNIQUE

Dip-dyeing and eraser stamp

MATERIALS

Plain white cotton duvet cover and pillowcase

PRINTING TOOLS

Rubber gloves

Fabric dye for hand use in main color

Fabric paint in contrast color

Large bucket or plastic crate

Washing line or chair

Newspaper

Sponge

Pencil eraser

1 Wearing rubber gloves, prepare your fabric dye according to the manufacturer's instructions in a bucket or plastic crate large enough to fit your duvet cover without it being too creased.

2 As the dyeing technique involves starting with part of the cover in the dye and then gradually lifting it out to achieve an ombre, or graded, dye effect, you need a way of suspending the duvet cover in the dye. A washing line is ideal for this.

3 Wash and spin-dry your duvet cover and pillowcase and leave them damp before you start the dyeing process, then hang the duvet cover over your washing line or chair. Let's say that you want to leave ⅓ of the duvet cover undyed. Start by hanging it so approximately ⅔ of it is in the dye. Suspend the fabric there steadily for 20 minutes, then lift it out so just ⅓ is left soaking in the dye. Leave it there for a further 20 minutes, Finally, lift it out so only the last 6in (15cm) or so is left in the dye. Leave it for a further 20 minutes.

4 Remove your duvet cover from the dye and rinse out the excess dye under running water. I used a hose in the garden but you could also transfer the duvet cover carefully to a sink. Wring out, then dry gently to avoid dripping. Be very careful not to get any of the color on the undyed parts of the duvet. Once the water runs clear, wash the duvet cover in the washing machine. Make sure it is dry and ironed before you start to print.

5 To dye the pillowcase, dye the whole thing, leaving it in the dye solution for 40 minutes and stirring it around occasionally. Then rinse, wash, dry, and iron it.

6 The design is applied using the stamp technique on page 12. To print the duvet cover, lay it out on a flat surface with some newspaper inside between the top and bottom layers so the paint doesn't come through.

7 Load a pencil eraser with fabric paint using a sponge, then use this to build up clusters of dots, gradually applying fewer dots as you reach the undyed area of the duvet cover. For the pillowcase, line with newspaper and simply print dots all over.

8 Once you are happy with your design, iron the printed areas to set the paint and you are ready to enjoy your new bedlinen.

3

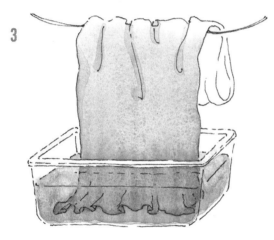

7

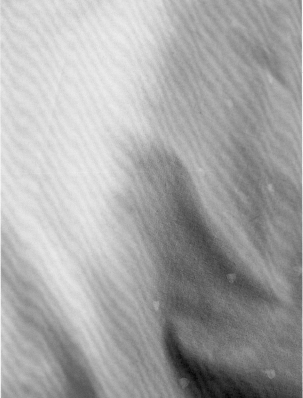

PRINTING TIPS

Dip-dyeing can be a bit messy, so be careful. I did mine outside so I could use a washing line to suspend the fabric in the dye. Embrace the imperfections that you will inevitably get—they make every piece unique.

PHOTO PATCHWORK QUILT

You can make a memory quilt from old family photos or from images of special places you have visited. Pick images with similar coloring or use your computer to adjust them. Match the rest of your patchwork pieces to this color theme.

PRINTING TECHNIQUE

Photo transfer

MATERIALS

Fabric (white or cream cotton fabric), you will need approx. 40 x 40in (102 x 102cm) in total for the front:

Cut 16 photo squares, 6 x 6in (15 x 15cm)

Cut 4 quilt edging strips, 32½ x 2½in (82 x 6cm)

Sufficient fabric to make 32 printed side strips and 16 corner squares (see instructions)

Backing fabric: 32½ x 32½in (82 x 82cm)

Scissors, pins, needle, matching thread, tape measure

PRINTING TOOLS

Computer

Inkjet printer

Letter-sized (A4) sheets of Inkjet photo transfer paper: 8+

1 This design is applied using the photo transfer technique on page 17. For this project you will need 16 photographic images, You can use the photo-editing software on your computer to adjust the color and size of your images. Each one must be 5½ x 5½in (14 x 14cm). Use your computer to reverse the images, then print them on inkjet photo transfer paper. The images will be the right way around when you transfer them to the fabric.

2 Cut out the 16 photo squares from your fabric and iron them flat. Cut out each printed image, leaving a ½in (1cm) border of photo transfer paper around each one.

3 Place a paper image face down on a fabric square and, following the instructions that came with your photo transfer paper, iron your transfer in place and peel away the backing. Repeat to make 16 fabric photo squares.

PRINTING TIPS

Photo transfers will print back to front, so remember to reverse your images before transferring them to the fabric. Take care when ironing the seams as the phototransfers do not like direct heat.

3

5

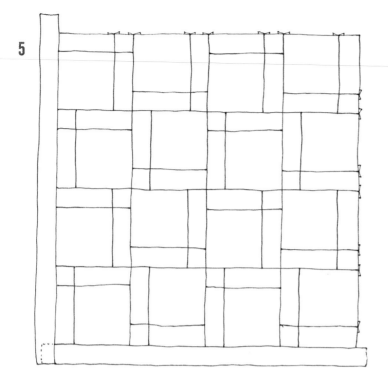

6

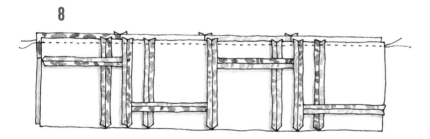

8

4 Each photo square on the quilt is surrounded by pieces of printed fabric. For these, either use printed offcuts from other projects or print pieces of fabric specially using any technique you like from this book. Either way, you must end up with 32 printed side strips, each measuring 2½ x 6in (6 x 15cm) and 16 corner squares, each measuring 2½ x 2½in (6 x 6cm). Iron all your fabric to make it easier to line up the edges when constructing the quilt.

5 When sewing the quilt together, think of it as 16 large squares, each made up of four pieces—the photo square, two side strips and a corner square.

6 Leaving a ½in (1cm) seam allowance, first join a corner square to a side strip and a side strip to the photo square. Finally, join the corner square with its side strip to the photo square with its side strip. Follow the illustration to check how to make up the large squares.

7 Press all the seams open on the wrong side as you work, taking care not to iron directly on the phototransfers as ironing will damage them.

8 Once all 16 large squares are ready, sew them together in rows to make four strips, each consisting of four squares. Again, leave a ½in (1cm) seam allowance and press all the seams open on the wrong side.

PRINTING TIPS

For the printed panels of fabric, try to stick to two or three colors that complement each other, or you can really get creative and use as many colors as you like!

9 Now join the four strips together to make one big panel. Once again, leave a ½in (1cm) seam allowance and press all the seams open on the wrong side.

10 To finish your quilt, sew an edging strip to each side. Position the first strip along one side, right side to right side, leaving ½in (1cm) spare at the top and a 2in (5cm) overhang at the bottom. Sew them together leaving a ½in (1cm) seam allowance. When you join the next strip, attach it to the 2in (5cm) overhang to create a neat, square corner.

11 Continue adding edging strips in this way until you have a square quilt measuring 32½ x 32½in (82 x 82cm). Press all the seams open on the wrong side.

12 To attach the backing fabric, lay it on top of the quilt, right side to right side. Pin it in place. Leaving a ½in (1cm) seam allowance, sew around all four sides. Leave a small opening in one edge for turning.

13 Trim the corners (see page 115) and turn the quilt to the right side through the opening. Push out all the corners from the inside and press the edges. Hand-sew the opening closed, then topstitch a neat line of stitches all the way around to finish the quilt.

HOT WATER BOTTLE COVER

Who doesn't love to snuggle up with a hot water bottle on a chilly evening? The print I've devised is a cute forest scene. I like to think that the footprints were made by a cuddly bear.

1 This design is applied using the eraser stamp technique on page 12. Prepare your stamps using the tree and footprint motifs on page 121. Cut out your main fabric pieces using the templates on page 123.

2 Load each stamp with one of the fabric paints using a sponge and build up your two-color design on the main fabric by stamping it all over with footprints and trees. Practice first on a scrap of fabric until you are confident you can achieve a clean, clear print.

3 To make the little tag on the side of the cover, cut out a piece of the main fabric so it is big enough when folded to accommodate a single footprint on each side.

4 When you are happy with your design, iron the fabric to set the paint. Use a low heat setting to avoid shrinking the felt.

5 Next cut out your lining fabric pieces using the templates on page 123.

6 Before you can make up the hot water bottle, you must attach the Velcro® fastening that will close the cover on the back. Working with the top back piece of lining fabric right side up, sew the hooked (rougher) strip of Velcro® 2in (5cm) from the long edge and centered on it.

7 Working with the bottom back piece of main fabric right side up, sew the looped (softer) strip of Velcro® 2½in (6cm) from the top edge, as marked on the template, and centered. Make sure the two strips of Velcro® line up.

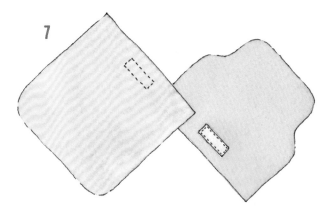

LEVEL:

PRINTING TECHNIQUE
Eraser stamp

MATERIALS
Fabric template on page 123

Main fabric (fleece or felt):

Front piece: cut one, 38 x 26cm (15 x 10in)

Top back piece: cut one, 24 x 26cm (9½ x 10in)

Bottom back piece: cut one, 26 x 26cm (10 x 10in)

Tag: extra scrap

Lining fabric:

Front piece: cut one, 38 x 26cm (15 x 10in)

Top back piece: cut one, 24 x 26cm (9½ x 10in)

Bottom back piece: cut one, 26 x 26cm (10 x 10in)

Velcro® strip: 2½in (6cm)

Scissors

Pins, matching thread

PRINTING TOOLS
Print motifs on page 121

2 large erasers

Wooden or acrylic backing block

Glue

Lino cutter

Craft knife

Fabric paint in two colors

Sponge

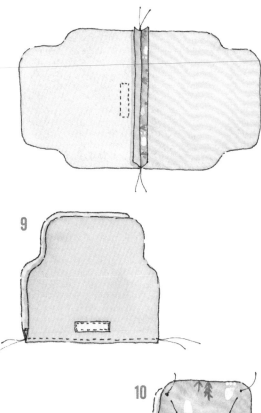

8 Next, you must sew the lining to each of the back pieces. Lay the top back piece of lining fabric on the top back piece of main fabric, right sides together. Leaving a ½in (1cm) seam allowance, sew along the long edge, where you just attached the Velcro®. Turn to the right side and press the seam flat, then topstitch close to the folded edge. Now you have your lining attached to the top back piece.

9 Repeat with the bottom pieces, placing the lining and main fabrics right sides together. Again, sew along the long edge. Turn to the right side and press the seam flat, then topstitch close to the folded edge. Now you have your lining attached to the bottom back piece.

10 To make life easier and stop your lining fabric moving around as you make up the cover, you need to tack the front piece of lining to the front piece of the main fabric. Lay one on top of the other, wrong sides together, and roughly tack them together with a large cross. This makes your lined front piece.

11 Fold the tag across its width, right side to right side. Sew around the sides and bottom, very close to the edge. Turn the tag to the right side through the open end.

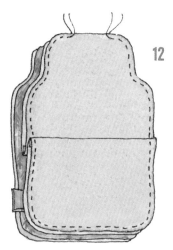

12 Now you can join all the pieces to make the cover. Start by joining the Velcro® strips to create one complete back piece. Next, lay the back on the front with the right sides of the main fabric facingeach other. Pin in place. To attach the tag, slip it, pointing inward, between the main fabric front and bottom back panels. Make sure you catch it in your line of sewing.

13 Leaving a ½in (1cm) seam allowance, sew all around the edge of the cover. Go carefully where the pieces overlap as the layers will be very thick and harder to sew through. Trim the seam allowance to ¼in (0.5cm), turn right side out, and press.

BERRY LAVENDER BAGS

These pretty little lavender bags will freshen up any space. Hang them in your closet or bathroom to keep your clothes and towels smelling fresh and clean. You could substitute any fragrant dried flowers to match your home and your taste.

LEVEL:

PRINTING TECHNIQUE

Foam stamp

MATERIALS, PER BAG

Main fabric:

Front and back: cut two, 6 x 4in (14.5 x 10cm)

Muslin panel: 2 x 4in (5 x 10cm)

Dried lavender: 1¾oz (50g)

Ribbon: ¼ x 4in (5mm x 10cm)

Small button, needle, matching thread

PRINTING TOOLS

Print motifs on page 120

Foam sheets

Craft knife

Scissors

Wooden or acrylic backing blocks

Glue

Fabric paint

Sponge

PRINTING TIPS

This cute little design is made up
of two layered prints: the stems and
the berries. You can play with the
positioning and overlay the stamps
to get three different designs.

1 Iron your fabric and cut it to size.

2 The design is applied using the foam stamp technique on
page 13. Prepare your stamps using the stem and berry
motifs on page 120.

3 First load the stem stamp with fabric paint using a sponge.
You will be printing just one of the pieces of main fabric to
make the front of the bag. Only print in the lower part of the fabric
as you will be adding a muslin panel above it later on. Practice first
on a scrap of fabric until you are confident you can achieve a
clean, clear print.

4 Build up the design by adding the berries. You could try out a
few different patterns.

5 When you are happy with your finished design, iron the fabric
to set the paint.

6 Now you are going to cut away a strip of the main fabric
and replace it with the muslin. This helps the lovely scent of
the lavender come through. To do this, cut across your printed
piece 4in (10cm) from the bottom. This leaves you with a 4 x 4in
(10 x 10cm) square of printed fabric and a 1¾ x 4in (4.5 x 10cm)
piece of unprinted fabric. Put the unprinted fabric to one side.

7 Now match the long edge of the muslin strip to the top of the
printed square, with right sides together. Leaving a ¼in (5mm)
seam allowance, sew the two together.

3

7

8 Turn to the wrong side and press the seam allowance toward the printed fabric. On the right side, topstitch very close to the folded edge of the printed fabric. This tidies the raw edges and adds a decorative touch.

9 Measure and mark 1½in (4cm) from this seam along the muslin. Rejoin the piece of unprinted fabric at this mark, leaving a ¼in (5mm) seam allowance. Turn to the wrong side and press the seam allowance toward the thicker fabric. Topstitch as above.

10 Lay the three-part front on top of the back piece, right sides together. Trim the top of the front piece until the front and back are the same length. Leaving a ¼in (5mm) seam allowance, sew the front and back together. Leave a small opening along one edge for turning the bag and stuffing it.

11 Turn the bag to the right side through the opening and press. Add the lavender through the opening, then handsew the opening closed. Stitch a loop of ribbon and a decorative button to the top. Your bag is now ready to hang.

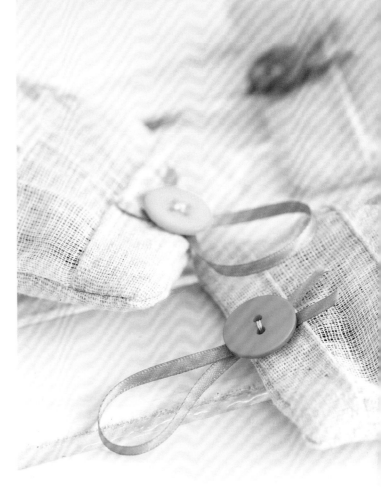

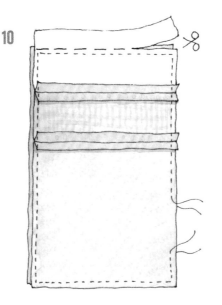

COVERED STORAGE BOX

You can transform any box into stylish storage to complement your home decor. Why not make a set of different-sized boxes to hide all your clutter away?

LEVEL:

PRINTING TECHNIQUE

Paper doily stencil

MATERIALS

Fabric (see instructions)

Box (either a shop-bought storage box, a shoe box, or another sturdy box)

PRINTING TOOLS

Paper doilies in various sizes (at least 6)

Stencil brush

Fabric paint

Paintbrush

Water-based glue

1 Remove any handles or other details, such as metal label holders. You will reattach those at the end.

2 Measure the length of each side of your box and add these measurements together. Add 8in (20cm) to the total—this is the fabric for the overlap—to give you the length of fabric you will need. Now measure the height of the sides, and again add 8in (20cm) to your measurements. This gives you the measurement for the depth of fabric you will need.

3 If your box has a lid, measure the top of the lid in exactly the same way. Add 4in (10cm) to these dimensions.

4 Iron your fabric, cut it to the sizes needed for the box and the lid, and lay it on a flat surface ready for printing.

5 This design is applied using the stencil technique on page 14. You will need at least 6 doilies as they will get a bit clogged up with paint as you work. Start to stencil lightly through the doilies, using the stencil brush to push the paint through the holes. I printed simple semicircles and overlapped them to make my design, but you could choose other layouts such as the whole circle of the doily or just small sections closely overlapped. Experiment and practice first on a scrap of fabric until you are confident you can achieve a clean, clear print.

6 When you are happy with your finished design and all the fabric has been printed, iron the fabric to set the paint.

7 Start by attaching the fabric to one of the long sides of the box, leaving a bit of fabric for the overlap at the starting end. Now continue around the first short side, then the second long side, and finish at the second short side. Using the paintbrush, coat each side with glue as you get to it. Smooth the fabric in place, pulling it tight to avoid air bubbles.

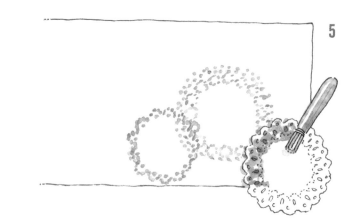

5

8 Fold over and glue a narrow hem along the end of the fabric to enclose the raw edge. Glue this folded edge neatly in place over the overlap at the starting end so you have a tidy corner.

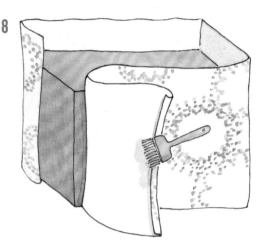

9 Now you will fold the fabric over, gift-wrap style, so it also covers the bottom of the box. Apply glue to the bottom of the box then fold in the fabric along the two short sides and press it in place. Now fold in the fabric along the two long sides, making neat miters at the corners. Glue the fabric in place. When you fold in the fabric along the second long side, first fold over and glue a narrow hem, to enclose the raw edge. Allow to dry before moving on to the top edge.

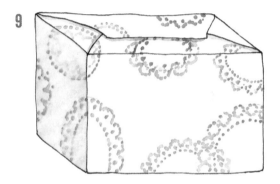

10 For the top edge of the box, trim the fabric if necessary so you have a neat 2in (5cm) overlap. Top up the glue along the top edge and continue it over the edge and onto the first 2in (5cm) of the inside of the box. Fold over the fabric to the inside, securing it in place.

11 Use this same process to cover the lid of your box, but this time start by gluing the top of the lid first. Take care on the inside corners to make sure the fabric isn't too bulky there or your lid won't fit back on.

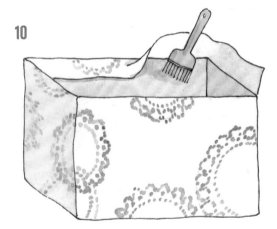

12 Reattach any labels or label holders to your box, and you're done.

PRINTING TIPS

This is a simple idea that uses store-bought paper doilies as stencils; they are available from most supermarkets and from cake or party stores. Make sure you try out different patterns as some work better than others. Some doilies are too delicate and the stenciling doesn't come through very clearly—you need doilies with a nice, simple, cut pattern.

FABRIC-COVERED NOTEBOOK

Customize any notebook by covering it in your own hand-printed fabric—perfect for a gift or to jazz up your studies.

PRINTING TECHNIQUE

Foam stamp

MATERIALS

Fabric: 16 x 12in (40 x 30cm)

6 x 8in (A5) notebook

Tailor's chalk

PVA glue or glue stick

Stiff piece of card or glue spreader

Scissors

2 pieces of card, 7 x 4½in (18 x 11cm)

PRINTING TOOLS

Print motifs on page 121

Foam sheets

Craft knife

Scissors

Placemat or wooden board, for backing block

Glue

Fabric paint in 2 or 3 colors

Sponge

1 Iron your fabric. Measure the notebook you plan to cover and cut out your fabric so there is at least a 2in (5cm) border to spare all around the edges. The measurements I have used here will work for an 6 x 8in (A5) notebook. Lay the fabric on a flat surface ready for printing.

2 The design is applied using the foam stamp technique on page 13, but instead of mounting the stamps on individual wooden or acrylic backing blocks, use the glasses motifs on page 121 to cut three stamps. Mount all three, one above the other, on an old placemat or a wooden board.

3 Carefully plan and mark the fabric with tailor's chalk where you want to print. Load the stamp with fabric paint using a sponge. You can use a different shade of paint on each motif at the same time (I've used three) if you're very careful not to smudge them. Practice first on a scrap of fabric until you are confident you can achieve a clean, clear print.

PRINTING TIPS

Be careful with your placement—trace the book shape onto the fabric in chalk before you print so you can get it right in the center of the front cover.

4 Leave the paint to dry, then iron to set the paint.

5 Place the fabric, printed side facing down, on a clean, flat surface. Open your notebook, lay it on the fabric and use chalk to mark the edges of the notebook. Make sure the printed design is correctly centered on the front cover.

6 Remove the notebook and coat its spine and front cover with a thin, even layer of PVA glue, applied with a stiff piece of card or glue spreader, or use a glue stick. Return the notebook to the fabric, press the notebook to the fabric, and smooth the back of the front cover to remove any bubbles and creases. Repeat this process with the back cover.

7 Next you need to fold over the excess fabric to create a neat finish. Start at the spine. If there is a gap between the spine of your notebook and the pages, carefully snip either side of the spine, top and bottom to make a little tab, then tuck the tab down into the gap.

8 If there isn't a gap, just neatly cut either side of the spine, then snip off the excess.

9 Spread a layer of glue along the edges of the back cover and fold the fabric over, smoothing it down as you go. When you reach the corners, add a little extra glue and, just like wrapping a present, fold the fabric inward to form a little triangle. Then fold it over again to make a neat corner.

10 Repeat this process on the front cover, then leave the glue to dry completely.

11 Finish by coating the back of each piece of card with glue and sticking them over the front and back inside covers to conceal the edges of the fabric.

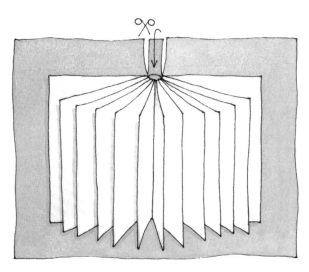

7

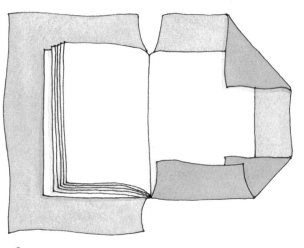

9

IKAT-PRINT PINBOARD

Recycle a decorative frame to make this quick and easy useful pinboard project. Look for frames in thrift stores that could be painted and brought back to life to match your decor.

PRINTING TECHNIQUE

Fruit and vegetable print

MATERIALS

Decorative frame, painted if required

Fabric: 2in (5cm) larger all round than the opening in your frame

Thick card

Spray adhesive

Masking tape

Drawing pins

Buttons

Superglue

Scissors

PRINTING TOOLS

2 oval-shaped potatoes

Kitchen knife

Fabric paint in two colors

Sponge

1 Measure your frame, iron your fabric, and cut it out so it is 2in (5cm) larger than the frame all round. Lay the fabric on a flat surface for printing.

2 The design is applied using the potato print technique on page 11. Practice first on a scrap of fabric until you are confident you can achieve a clean, clear print. Choose two oval-shaped potatoes, one larger than the other. Carve the larger potato to make an oval ring with jagged edges (see photo opposite for guidance, and the smaller one to make an oval block that fits inside the ring.

3 Load the oval ring first with one of the fabric paints using a sponge, then print in vertical columns the length of the fabric, staggering the columns in a brick pattern.

4 Now load the oval block with the other fabric paint and use it to print inside every other ring. When you are happy with your finished design, iron your fabric to set the paint.

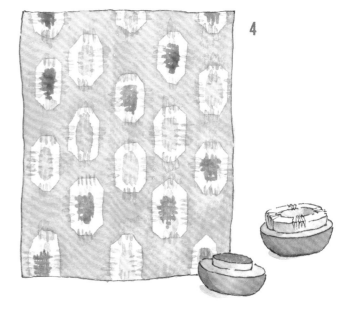

4

5 Next you need to cut a piece of thick card to the exact size of your frame, then stick your printed fabric to the front of the card using spray adhesive. Smooth the surface of the fabric so there are no lumps or bumps.

6 Turn the card over and fold the overlapping edges of the fabric down onto the back of the card. Tape the edges in place using masking tape.

7 Place the fabric-covered card into the frame and reattach the back of the frame.

8 To make your button pins, simply superglue drawing pins to the back of your buttons and allow to dry.

6

8

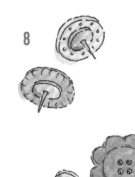

PRINTING TIPS

I created this ikat pattern using the humble potato, chipping away at the edges and center to get the jagged effect. Look for inspiration in the shapes of the potatoes in your vegetable basket.

IRONING BOARD COVER

Spruce up your old ironing board with a new handprinted cover. This colorful print will brighten up a dull chore—you'll be steaming ahead before you know it!

LEVEL: 🐦

PRINTING TECHNIQUE

Eraser stamp and toilet-roll tube print

MATERIALS

Fabric: (to fit small and medium ironing boards), 59 x 20in (1.5 x 50cm)

Newspaper

Clear adhesive tape

Pencil

Tailor's chalk

Elastic or strong thin cord, approx. ½ x 80in (1cm x 2m)

Wadding (optional)

Pins, safety pin, matching thread

PRINTING TOOLS

Large eraser

Lino cutter

Craft knife

Cardboard toilet-roll tube

Fabric paint in 2 colors

Sponge

Hairdryer (optional)

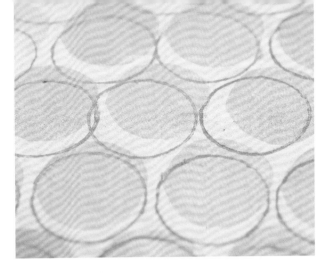

1 Before you begin, you need to make a paper template of your ironing board. Use clear adhesive tape to join together pieces of newspaper into a long strip, then lay your ironing board upside down on top. Draw around the ironing board, then draw another line 4in (10cm) from the first.

2 Iron your fabric and cut it into a rectangle a little larger than your template. You will cut the fabric to size later. Lay the fabric on a flat surface ready for printing.

3 The design is applied using the eraser stamp technique on page 12, with outline circles layered on top using a cardboard toilet-roll tube. Prepare a simple solid circle stamp using a large eraser, you can use your toilet-roll tube as a template. To print, load the stamp with fabric paint using a sponge. Use this to print circles across the fabric in rows. You can mark out your rows with a chalk line or print freehand. Leave the paint to dry. If you like, you can use a hairdryer to speed this up. Now print outline circles on top, using the end of a cardboard toilet-roll tube dipped in contrasting fabric paint. Practice first on a scrap of fabric until you are confident you can achieve a clean, clear print.

4 When you are happy with your finished design, iron the fabric to set the paint.

5 Now lay your paper template on top of the printed fabric and cut the fabric to size. Turn the edge of the fabric in all around by ½in (1cm) and press, then, starting in the center of the short, straight side, fold the fabric over again by 1¼in (3cm). Pin, then sew along the first fold to make the channel for your elastic or cord.

6 Use a safety pin attached to the end to thread your elastic or cord through the channel, leaving a long tail at each end.

7 Place your ironing board cover over your ironing board and pull the elastic or cord until you have a nice tight fit. Tie the ends to secure. If needed, you could add a layer of wadding under your new cover. Simply cut out the wadding using your template and place it on the ironing board under your new cover.

PRINTING TIPS

This simple design uses a toilet-roll tube to build up rows of circles. Simply dip and print!

3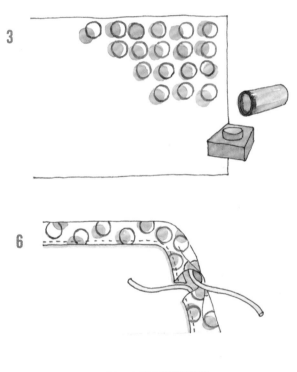

6

7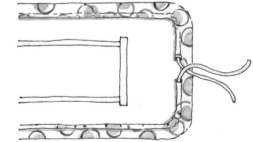

LAUNDRY BAG

A simple drawstring bag like this has many uses. It's ideal for hiding your laundry or for keeping your socks and underwear sorted. It hangs neatly on the back of a door or over the end of the bedstead.

LEVEL: 🐦 🐦

PRINTING TECHNIQUE

Lino print

MATERIALS

Fabric: cut two, 18 x 28in (46 x 71cm), plus an extra scrap for the tag

Cotton tape or cord: ½in x 10ft (1 x 300cm)

Matching thread

PRINTING TOOLS

Print motifs on page 122

Lino

Lino cutter

Craft knife

Fabric paint in 2 colors

Sponge

1 This design is applied using the lino print technique on pages 12–13. Prepare your two lino blocks using the hydrangea flower and leaf motifs on page 122.

2 Iron your fabric, cut it to size and lay it on a flat surface ready for printing.

3 Load each stamp with fabric paint using a sponge. Practice first on a scrap of fabric until you are confident you can achieve a clean, clear print. Build up your design using the hydrangea first and fitting in the leaves around the printed hydrangeas. When you are happy with your finished design, iron the fabric to set the paint.

4 For the little tag on the side of the laundry bag, cut out a piece of fabric so it is big enough when folded to accommodate a single leaf print on each side.

1

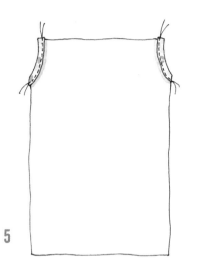

5

PRINTING TIPS

This hydrangea flower pattern is tricky to carve. Take your time and keep looking at the original design to make sure you don't carve away the wrong parts.

5 To make up the laundry bag, first you must make channels along the top to thread the cord through. Working on the wrong side of the fabric, fold the first 4in (10cm) of one long side inwards by ¼in (5mm). Press the folded edge, then sew it in place with a neat line of stitches. Repeat on the other long side, then repeat on the second piece of fabric.

6 Still with the wrong side of the fabric facing you, fold over the top edge by ½in (1cm), then fold it over a second time, this time by 4in (10cm). Press the folds flat, then sew a neat line of stitches close to the edge of the first fold to keep everything in place. Sew another line of stitches 1in (2.5cm) above the first line. This makes the channel for the drawstring. Repeat on the second piece of fabric.

7 To finish the little tag, fold its raw edges to the wrong side, then fold it again widthwise, enclosing all the raw edges. Press it and sew a neat line of stitches all the way around.

8 To make up the whole bag, work with right sides facing and match up the front and back pieces. Place the tag, pointing inward, between the layers at the bottom left-hand side. Pin the sides and bottom edge together. Leaving a ⅜in (7mm) seam allowance, sew the seams to create the bag shape. Make sure you catch the tag in your line of sewing. Stop your stitching short of the channel so you don't sew the channel closed.

9 Turn the whole bag right side out. Use a safety pin attached to one end of the cotton tape or cord to thread it through the channels. Tie the two ends of the tape or cord together and you're done.

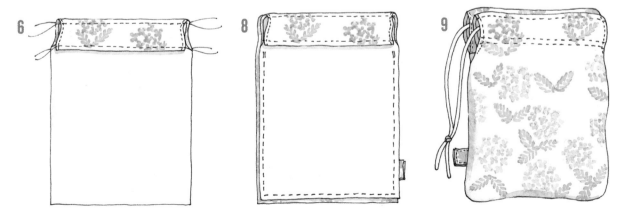

PINCUSHIONS

This gives you two pincushion projects in one. First there's the sewing machine pincushion—a clever way to have your pins always to hand by your machine. Then there's the jar pincushion. It's the perfect place to store your small craft essentials or your spare buttons and threads.

LEVEL: 🐦

PRINTING TECHNIQUE

Eraser stamp

MATERIALS

For the sewing machine pincushion:

Fabric: 6 x 6in (14.5 x 14.5cm)

Elastic: ½ x 12in (1 x 30cm)

Polyester stuffing

Needle, pins, matching thread

For the jar pincushion:

Fabric (sufficient to cover the jar's metal disc, plus extra to accommodate the stuffing; see text)

Mason jar

Pair of compasses

Scissors

Polyester stuffing

Hot-glue gun

Piece of card (optional)

PRINTING TOOLS

Print motif on page 120

1 large eraser

Lino cutter

Craft knife

Fabric paint in 3 colors

Sponge

Hairdryer (optional)

1 This design is applied using the eraser stamp technique on page 12. Prepare your stamp using the button motif on page 120.

2 To make the sewing machine pincushion, iron your fabric, and cut it to size. Load the stamp with fabric paint using a sponge and use it to print the fabric all over in a random pattern with a drop-shadow effect (see Printing Tips on page 109). Practice first on a scrap of fabric until you are confident you can achieve a clean, clear print.

3 When you are happy with your finished design, iron the fabric to set the paint.

4 Fold your square of fabric in half with right sides facing. Cut a piece of elastic long enough to go snugly around your sewing machine and pin the ends in place between the layers of fabric.

5 Leaving a ½in (1cm) seam allowance, sew all around the open sides. Secure the ends of the elastic in your stitching as you go. Leave a 2in (5cm) opening along the long side for turning the pincushion through.

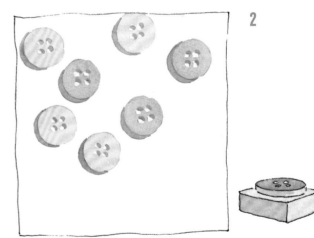

2

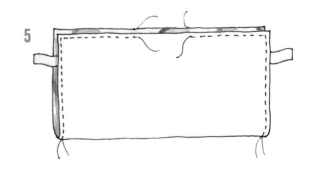

5

6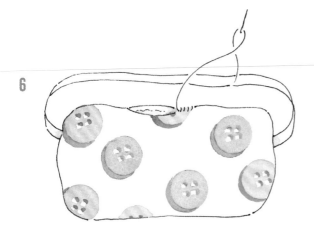

6 Pull the pincushion to the right side through the opening. Stuff it firmly with the stuffing, then sew the opening closed by hand.

7 Thread the elastic under the pressure foot of the sewing machine and position your pincushion where you can easily get to the pins.

8 The jar pincushion uses a Mason jar with a two-part top—a metal disc held in place by a metal band. Remove the metal band and disc and measure the radius of the disc. Set a pair of compasses 3in (8cm) longer than this measurement and use the compasses to draw a circle on your fabric.

9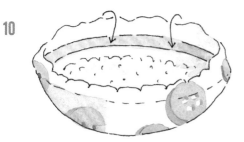

Print the fabric all over in a random pattern, as above, then iron the fabric to set the paint. Cut out the circle.

10 Now you are going to stuff and glue the fabric circle to the disc. I recommend using a hot-glue gun; the glue dries fast so you can stretch the fabric over the stuffing as you go. Lay out your fabric circle wrong side up. Place a handful of stuffing in the center, then lay the disc on top of the stuffing. Stretch the fabric up and around the stuffing and glue it in place all around the edge of the disc. You should have a shape that's a bit like a burger bun.

11 Trim the raw edges of the fabric to ½in (1cm) and glue them down.

12 Cut out a circle of spare fabric or card to cover the raw edges, then glue this on top, making it all neat.

13 Place a few small blobs of glue on the inside of the metal band, push the stuffing through the band, then screw the disc with its stuffing on the jar.

10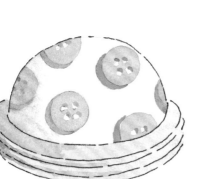

13

PRINTING TIPS

To get a 3-D, or drop-shadow effect, print in
a darker color first. Then, when the paint is
dry, overprint with white, slightly offsetting
the white print. You can use a hairdryer to
speed things up if you like.

SEWING MACHINE COVER

The perfect design for a pretty but practical sewing machine cover! One size fits all machines, keeps the dust away, and will look great in any craft room.

PRINTING TIPS

This cover is made up of three pieces of fabric. You'll be printing the main fabric with scissors and buttons, and the second fabric with cotton reels. See the printing tip on page 109 for advice on how to get a drop-shadow effect for the button prints.

LEVEL: 🐦🐦

PRINTING TECHNIQUE

Foam stamp and eraser stamp

MATERIALS

Main fabric:

Cut one, 11 x 32in (28 x 80cm)

Cut one, 4 x 32in (10 x 80cm)

Second fabric: cut one, 6 x 32in (15 x 80cm)

Lining fabric: cut one, 20 x 32in (50 x 80cm)

Cotton tape or ribbon: 1 x 40in (2.5cm x 1 metre), cut into 4 equal-sized lengths

Tailor's chalk

Pins, matching thread

PRINTING TOOLS

Print motifs on page 110

Foam sheets

Craft knife

Scissors

Wooden or acrylic backing block

Glue

2 large erasers

Lino cutter

Craft knife

Fabric paint in 3 colors

Sponge

Hairdryer (optional)

1 This design is applied using the foam stamp technique on page 13 for the scissor motif and the eraser stamp technique on page 12 for the buttons and cotton reel motifs. Prepare your stamps using the motifs on page 122.

2 Iron your main and second fabrics, cut them to size, and lay them on a flat surface ready for printing.

3 Start by printing the two pieces of your main fabric, using the scissors and button stamps. Load the scissors stamp with fabric paint using a sponge and print both pieces of main fabric in a uniform pattern. Now load the button stamp with fabric paint and stamp the buttons randomly—using a drop-shadow effect (see Printing Tips on page 109)—between the scissors. Practice first on a scrap of fabric until you are confident you can achieve clean, clear prints.

4 Mark diagonal lines on the second fabric using tailor's chalk. Load the cotton reel stamp with paint and print cotton reels along the diagonals. This gives a diamond pattern. When you are happy with your finished designs, iron the fabrics to set the paint.

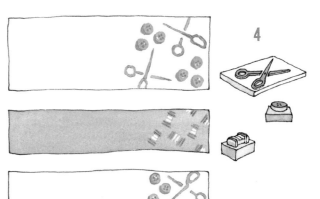

5 Now you are going to join all the pieces of fabric together, so the second fabric is between the two pieces of main fabric. Join them, right sides together, along their long edges. Sew, leaving a ½in (1cm) seam allowance. On the wrong side, press all the seams flat. For added strength and a nice crisp finish, neatly topstitch along the edges of the seams.

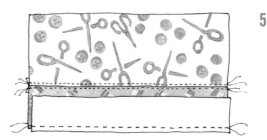

6 To join the printed fabric to the lining, lay the lining out flat and place the printed fabric on top, right sides together. Slide the ends of the four pieces of tape between the fabric and the lining along the long sides and about 7in (18cm) from each corner.

7 Pin everything in place, then sew around all four sides leaving a ½in (1cm) seam allowance. Secure the ends of the tape in your stitching as you go. Leave a small opening along one long side for turning.

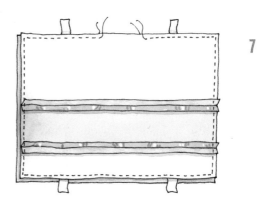

8 Trim off the seam allowance at the corners and turn the whole cover to the right side through the opening. Push out the corners and press the edges flat. Pin the opening closed, then topstitch a neat line of stitches close to the edge to finish.

JAPANESE FABRIC GIFTWRAP

A super cute and environmentally friendly way to wrap your gifts, you can make your wrapping to any size you need, but a simple square of fabric can work wonders and can be reused again and again.

LEVEL: 🐦

PRINTING TECHNIQUE

Household item print

MATERIALS

Fabric: 18 x 18in (46 x 46cm)

Pins, matching thread (optional)

PRINTING TOOLS

Print motifs on page 117

Wallpaper seam roller

Scraps of sticky-backed foam

Scissors or craft knife

Fabric paint

Sponge

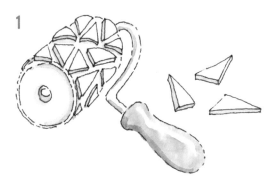

1 This design is applied using the household item print technique on page 11. In this case, it uses a wallpaper seam roller with simple triangle shapes stuck all over it. Using the print motifs on page 117, cut out a number of small triangle shapes in several different sizes from the sticky-backed foam. Stick these onto the roller, leaving small gaps between triangles.

2 Iron your fabric, cut it to size and lay it on a flat surface ready for printing. You need to be able to run the roller across the whole piece in one go.

3 Load the roller with fabric paint using a sponge. Practice first on a scrap of fabric until you are confident you can achieve a clean, clear print.

4 Start at one corner of the fabric and carefully run the roller across. As the roller runs out of paint, you'll notice that you get a natural fade. Use this in your design either by making sure you always run the roller across in the same direction or by alternating directions. If you always go the same way, one side of your fabric will look more faded, but if you alternate, you get a more obvious striped effect. Reload your roller with paint each time you roller across.

5 When you are happy with your finished design, iron the fabric to set the paint.

6 Either leave the edges of your fabric as they are, so they fray naturally, or, with the wrong side facing you, fold under the raw edges along all four sides and pin. Fold the fabric under a second time, so the raw edges are enclosed. Press the folds flat then sew a neat line of stitches close to the edge of the first fold to keep everything in place. Take care to stitch a neat right angle around the corners.

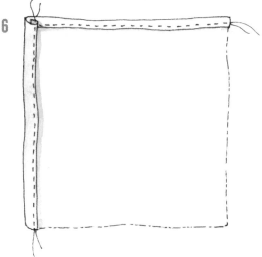

PRINTING TIPS

Using a roller with glued-on foam shapes is a great way to get a random pattern that can cover a large surface fast. You can vary your design by using different-colored paints and by making the most of the natural fade you get as you roll across the fabric.

BASIC SEWING TECHNIQUES

All the projects in this book are designed to be easy to achieve, no matter what your sewing skills. I have kept the sewing to its simplest and as long as you can sew a straight line, you should be more than capable of trying out all these projects. There are lots of new skills to learn as you work your way through them. Here are a few basic techniques you will need.

BASIC EQUIPMENT

- Sewing machine and zipper foot
- Sharp scissors
- Seam ripper
- Pins
- Safety pins
- Chalk / tailor's chalk
- Tape measure
- Large ruler
- Iron and ironing board

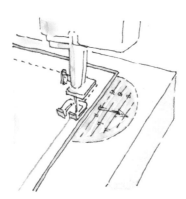

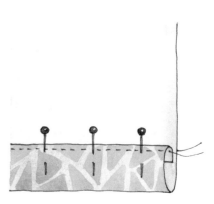

SEAM ALLOWANCE

The seam allowance is the distance between a seam and the edge of the fabric. There are many standard measurements for seam allowances but your pattern should always tell you what seam allowance to use. In this book I always use ½in (1cm) and all the measurements I give take this seam allowance into account. Occasionally I might ask you to use a narrower seam allowance, so always read the project text carefully.

SIMPLE SEAM

To sew two pieces of fabric together, line up the fabric with the right sides facing. Pin them together at regular intervals along the edge, then sew a straight line of stitches, following the edge of the fabric. Use the markings on your machine's needle plate to make sure you are sewing straight. Remove the pins as you sew. To turn a corner, insert the needle, raise the presser foot and turn the fabric. Lower the presser foot to continue. When you come to the end of your seam, use the reverse button on your machine and reverse stitch for about ½in (1cm) to stop the seam unraveling.

SIMPLE HEM

All the hems in this book are double hems—hems that completely enclose the raw edges. With the wrong side facing you, fold over the edge of the fabric by 1½in (1cm) along the line where you want your hem to be. Press a crisp edge, then fold the fabric over again by ½in (1cm). Press and pin in place. Sew a neat line of stitches very close to the edge of the second fold, removing the pins as you go.

SEWING A NEAT HEMMED CORNER

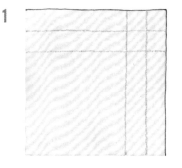

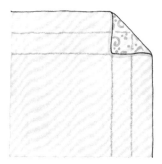

This is a simple and effective way to make neat hemmed right-angled corners for projects like napkins or tea towels. The simple folds enclose all the raw edges and reduce the bulky fabric at the corner. This principle works for a seam of any width; just adjust the measurements of the folds as required.

1 With the wrong side facing you, fold and press a ¼in (6mm) hem along both sides of the corner, then turn another ¼in (6mm) hem and press well again. Now unfold the fabric so you can see your foldlines.

2 Next, fold the point of the corner in so it meets the second set of foldlines. Press.

3 Fold a second time across the corner to enclose the raw edges and press again.

4 Now refold your sides along the first ¼in (6mm) foldline and press, then fold again along the second ¼in (6mm) foldline.

5 Your raw edges will all now be enclosed and the ends of the side seams should meet along a neat diagonal line. Sew the sides closed with a neat line of stitches close to the folded edge.

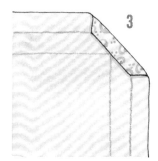

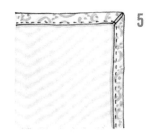

TRIMMING CORNERS AND CURVES

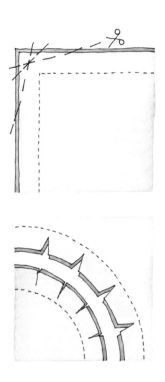

Once you have sewn your seams you need to trim them before you turn your project to the right side. This keeps the seams nice and crisp on the right side. To trim a right-angled corner, cut away the point of the corner on the diagonal, taking care not to cut through the stitches of your seams. When you turn the corner to the right side, it should have a lovely sharp point.

To trim an inside curve, cut away little triangles at regular intervals to reduce the bulk of the fabric, taking care not to cut through the stitches. For an outside curve, make straight cuts to allow the fabric to stretch more easily around the curve. When you turn the curved seam to the right side, it should lie nice and flat, without any wrinkles or puckers.

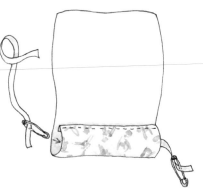

TOPSTITCHING

This is a decorative stitch that gives a neat finish to a project. I also sometimes use it to close an opening. On the right side, simply sew a neat line of straight stitches very close to the folded edge.

MAKING A TAG

A little printed tag in a side seam is a nice, professional-looking addition to any project. Start with a small oblong of fabric, twice the length of your finished tag, plus ¾in (2cm), and the width of your finished tag, plus ½in (1cm). With the right side facing you, fold and press the fabric in half widthwise. Print the tag with your motif on the right side near the foldline. Iron to set the paint, then open the strip out. With the wrong side facing you, fold a ¼in (6mm) hem along both long edges and press. With the right side facing you, refold the fabric widthwise so the folded edges meet, then sew two neat lines of stitches to join the folded edges. To attach the tag to your project, simply slip its open end, with the tag facing inward, between the layers of fabric as you sew them together to make the side seam.

THREADING CORD OR ELASTIC THROUGH A CHANNEL

To thread the end of your cord or elastic through a channel, attach a safety pin to one end of the cord. Insert the pin with the cord attached into one end of the channel. Use the pin to move the cord through the channel, holding onto the pin through the layers of fabric and pushing the pin forward as you pull the fabric backward, out of the way. Be careful not to lose your grip on the pin until it emerges far enough from the other side that you can hold onto the cord comfortably.

COVERING A BUTTON

If your project calls for a button, why not make a covered one? Two-part metal and plastic self-cover buttons are readily available in a variety of sizes. They consist of a top—the button part—and a back plate. To use, cut out a circle of fabric that is ½in (1cm) wider all around than the button. Handsew a line of running stitches around the outer edge of the fabric. Place the fabric, right side up, over the button top, and pull the stitches tight, gathering the fabric around the button as you go. Hold the fabric firmly in place and snap on the button's back plate.

MAKING FABRIC TIES AND HANDLES

Making fabric ties or handles is easy. Here I give you the general principles, but you should adjust all your measurements according to the width of your strip.

Start with a strip of fabric twice as wide as you want your finished tie or handle to be, plus ¾in (2cm). With the wrong side facing you, fold over and press a ½in (1cm) hem along both long edges of your strip. Now fold the strip lengthwise, wrong side to wrong side, so the two folded edges meet. Sew together with a neat line of stitches on the right side. Now sew another neat line of stitches along the other long edge of the strip to give you a neat, strong finish.

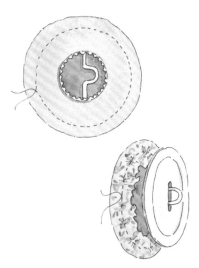

PRINT MOTIFS

All of these motifs are printed at half their actual size. They will need to be enlarged to 200%—using a photocopier—before use.

HONEYCOMB BUNTING (PAGE 18)

JAPANESE FABRIC GIFTWRAP (PAGE 112)

LEAF-FALL NAPKIN (PAGE 52)

TABLE RUNNER (PAGE 40)

QUILTED OVEN GLOVE (PAGE 42)

TIE-TOP
CURTAINS
(PAGE 20)

ROLLER BLIND (PAGE 26)

FEATHER-PRINT
POT HOLDER
(PAGE 61)

DOORSTOP CUBE (PAGE 34)

FULL-LENGTH APRON (PAGE 36)

LEAFY LAMPSHADE (PAGE 30)

BIRD-PRINT TEA
TOWEL (PAGE 48)

FERN-PRINT COASTERS
(PAGE 54)

CERAMIC DECAL PRINTING (PAGE 32)

STYLISH COT BUMPER (PAGE 73)

GIANT FLOOR CUSHIONS (PAGE 70)

PINCUSHIONS (PAGE 106)

BERRY LAVENDER
BAGS (PAGE 89)

VINE-LEAF PLACEMAT
(PAGE 50)

TEA COZY (PAGE 58)

BOLSTER CUSHION
(PAGE 66)

FABRIC-COVERED NOTEBOOKS
(PAGE 96)

HOT WATER
BOTTLE COVER
(PAGE 86)

WALL PRINT (PAGE 23)

SIMPLE ROUND
CUSHION (PAGE 76)

SEWING MACHINE COVER
(PAGE 110)

LAUNDRY BAG
(PAGE 104)

TEMPLATES

All of these templates—unless otherwise stated—are printed at half their actual size. They will need to be enlarged to 200% using a photocopier before use.

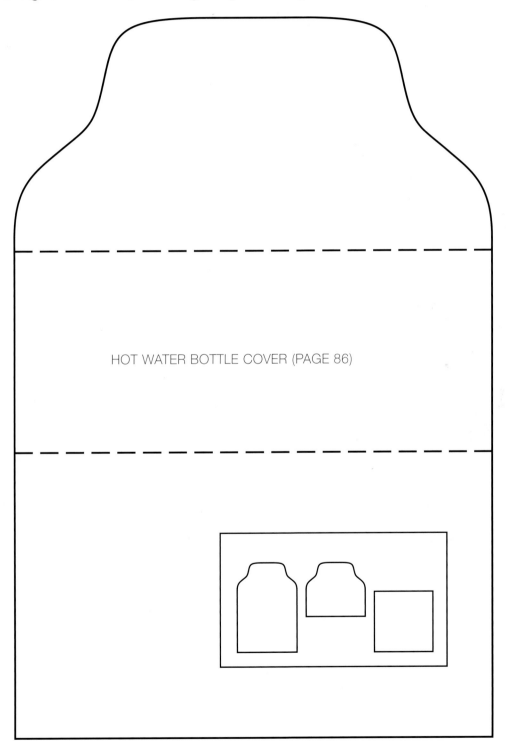

HOT WATER BOTTLE COVER (PAGE 86)

FULL-LENGTH APRON (PAGE 36)

The grid below indicates the size of this template—each square equals 2in. (5cm). Draw the apron up to its full size on paper. You may find it easier to use squared pattern paper to do this.

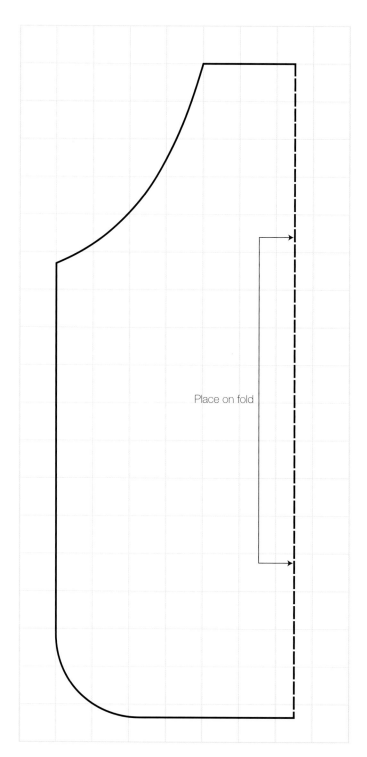

Place on fold

VINE-LEAF PLACEMAT (PAGE 50)—THIS TEMPLATE IS PRINTED AT FULL-SIZE

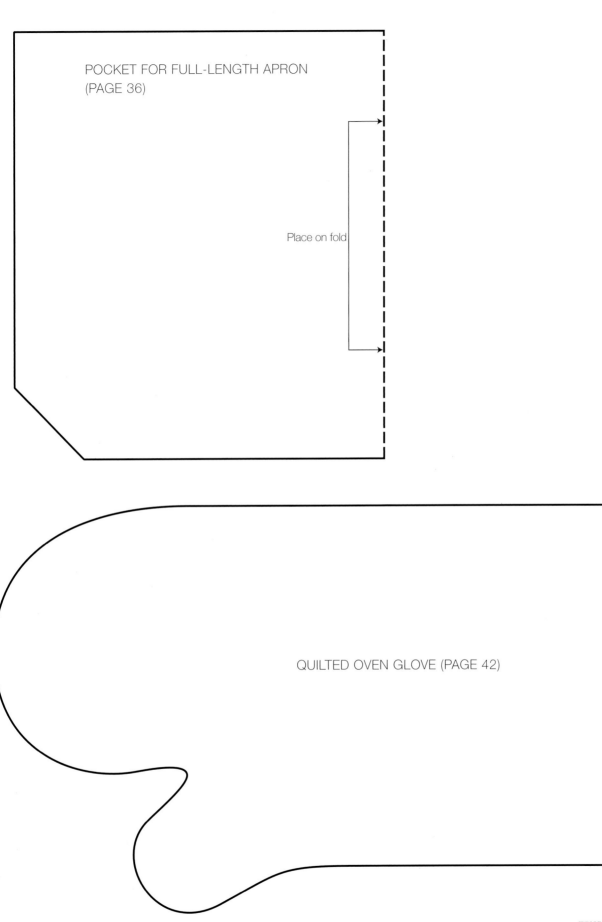

POCKET FOR FULL-LENGTH APRON
(PAGE 36)

Place on fold

QUILTED OVEN GLOVE (PAGE 42)

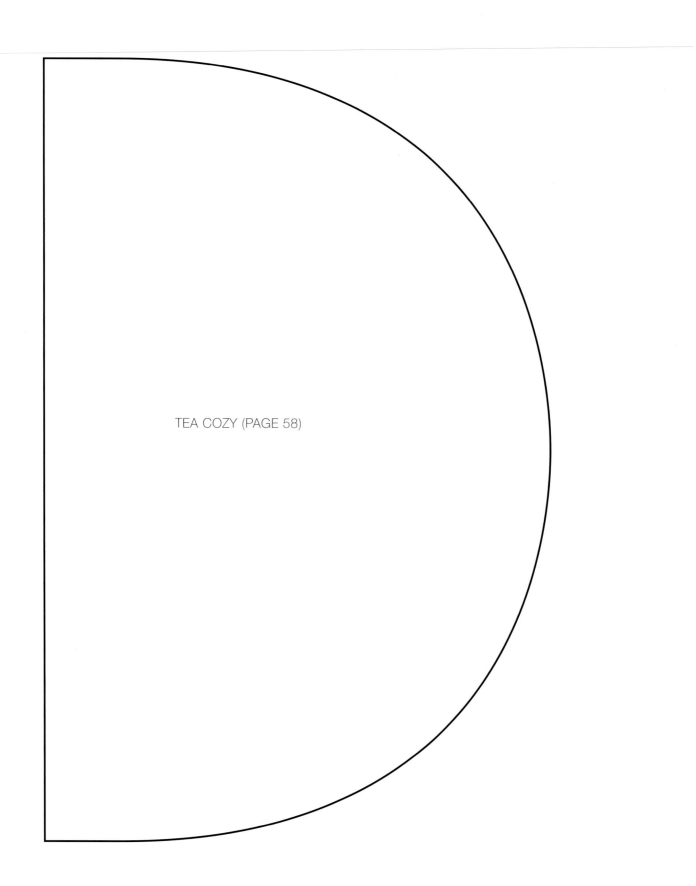

TEA COZY (PAGE 58)

SUPPLIERS

NORTH AMERICA

Art Shack
www.artshack.ca
Canadian supplier of arts and crafts
materials and equipment

Dharma Trading Co.
1604 Fourth St.
San Rafael, CA 94901 USA
+1 (800) 542–5227
www.dharmatrading.com
Textile craft supplies

Ebay.com
You can find all the printing equipment you
need here

Fabric Land
www.fabricland.ca
Large selection of fabrics, with stores
across Canada

Hobby Lobby
+1 (800) 888–0321
www.shop.hobbylobby.com
Online arts and crafts store with branches
across the US

Joann's
+1 (888) 739–4120
www.joann.com
Wide range of fabrics and haberdashery,
with stores across the USA

Michael's
Tel: +1 (800) 642–4235
www.michaels.com
Arts and crafts supplier with stores
across the USA and Canada

Rex Art
+1 (800) 739–2782
www.rexart.com
Arts and crafts supplies and materials

UNITED KINGDOM

Abakhan Fabrics, Hobby & Home
111–115 Oldham Street
Manchester
M4 1LN
+44 (0) 161 839 3229
enquiries@abakhan.co.uk
www.abakhan.co.uk
Fabric store

Art2ScreenPrint
Greenway, Hollywood Lane
West Kingsdown
Kent
TN15 6JG
+44 (0) 1474 850559
sales@art2screen.co.uk
www.art2screen.co.uk
Screen printing equipment

The Cloth House
47 Berwick Street,
London
W1F 8SJ
+44 (0) 20 7437 5155
www.clothhouse.com
Fabrics, vintage buttons, and braids

Ebay.co.uk
You can find all the printing equipment you
need here

Fred Aldous Ltd
37 Lever Street
Manchester
M1 1LW
+44 (0) 161 236 4224
support@fredaldous.zendesk.com
www.fredaldous.co.uk
Craft materials and fabric paint

George Weil & Sons
Old Portsmouth Road
Peasmarsh
Guildford
Surrey
GU3 1LZ
+44 (0) 1483 565800
esales@georgeweil.com
www.georgeweil.com
Rubber carving blocks and craft supplies

Handprinted.co.uk
+44 (0) 1243 697 606
www.handprinted.co.uk
Online printing supplier

John Lewis
+44 (0) 20 7629 7711
www.johnlewis.com
Department store with branches across
the UK; haberdashery and large range
of fabrics

Rainbow Silks
85 High Street
Great Missenden
Bucks
HP16 0AL
+44 (0)1494 862929
caroline@rainbowsilks.co.uk
www.rainbowsilks.co.uk
Wide range of silk fabrics

T N Lawrence & Son Ltd
208 Portland Road
Hove
East Sussex
BN3 5HR
+44 (0) 1273 260260
www.lawrence.co.uk
Printing suppliers

INDEX

ACKNOWLEDGMENTS

I would like to say a huge thank you to everyone who helped make this book happen. All the lovely people at CICO Books—Sally Powell, Anna Galkina, and Cindy Richards. Hilary Mandelberg for being such a fantastic and patient editor, Carrie Hill for the beautiful illustrations, Louise Leffler for the gorgeous design and Emma Mitchell for photographing my projects so well. Thank you also to Nel Haynes for styling the shots. Special thanks to Charlotte Done and Lucy Pass for helping me with design ideas and keeping my wine glass topped up! And finally, thanks to my children for being my inspiration and my toughest but best critics—love you guys xxx